SAMS
Teach Yourself

C++

Jesse Liberty

in 10 Minutes
SECOND EDITION

800 East 96th St., Indianapolis, Indiana, 46240 USA

Sams Teach Yourself C++ in 10 Minutes, Second Edition

Copyright © 2002 by Sams Publishing

International Standard Book Number: 0-672-32425-3

Library of Congress Catalog Card Number: 2002104735

Printed in the United States of America

First Printing: June 2002

09   11 10 9

Trademarks

Warning and Disclaimer

EXECUTIVE EDITOR
Michael Stephens

ACQUISITIONS EDITOR
Carol Ackerman

DEVELOPMENT EDITOR
Michael Watson

MANAGING EDITOR
Charlotte Clapp

PROJECT EDITOR
Matthew Purcell

PRODUCTION EDITOR
Matt Wynalda

INDEXER
Lisa Wilson

TECHNICAL EDITOR
Christopher McGee

TEAM COORDINATOR
Lynne Williams

INTERIOR DESIGNER
Gary Adair

COVER DESIGNER
Aren Howell

PAGE LAYOUT
Susan Geiselman

GRAPHICS
Steve Adams
Tammy Graham
Oliver Jackson
Laura Robbins

Contents

Introduction 1

1 Getting Started   5

The Mission 5
The C++ Language 6
Preparing to Program 7
C++, ANSI C++, Windows, and Other Areas of Confusion 7
Your Compiler and Editor 8
The Development Cycle 9
Evolving the Program 10
A Simple Program 10
Parts of the Program 11
Compile-Time Errors 12
Summing Up 13

2 Output to the Console—Standard Output   14

Enhancing the Empty Program 14
The `#include`, Character by Character 15
Namespaces 16
Comments 17
Whitespace 17
Functions 17
The `cout` Statement, Word by Word 18
Summing Up 19

3 Calculations   20

Performing and Displaying a Calculation 20
Nesting Parentheses 22
Using an Input Stream 22
Using `int` Variables and Constants 25
Types of Variables and Valid Names 27
Summing Up 29

4 Numeric Input   30

Numeric Input 30
What Went Wrong? 33
Summing Up 35

5 if Statements and Program Decisions   36

Dealing with a Failed Input Stream 36
Summing Up 41

6 Exception Handling   42

Exception Handling—A Better Way 42
Why Use Exceptions? 45
Summing Up 45

7 Functions   46

What Is a Function? 46
Defining Functions 47
Breaking the Example into Functions 48
Refactoring 53
Where You Put Function Code 54
Global Variables 55
Testing 56
Summing Up 56

8 Separating Code into Modules   57

What Is a Module? 57
Why Use a Module? 58
Making a Library Changes Your Names 60
Calling the Functions 62
Compiling Separately 64
Testing 65
Summing Up 65

9 do/while Loops   66

Where You Are 66
Doing Things More Than Once 66
Doing Things at Least Once 67

Doing Things Zero or More Times 71

Summing Up 72

10   Nested Loops and Complex bool Expressions   73

Nesting Loops 73

Relational Operators 75

Simplifying by Using a bool Variable 78

Summing Up 80

**11   switch Statements, static Variables, and
runtime_errors   81**

switch Statements 81

Generalizing the Calculator 82

Dealing with the New Exception 86

Summing Up 87

**12   Arrays, Loops, and the Increment and
Decrement Operators   88**

Using an Array to Create a Calculator Tape 88

The Tape 89

The for Loop 91

Writing Past the End of an Array 92

Incrementing and Decrementing 92

The Calculator Tape in the Accumulator 93

Summing Up 94

13   Storage: Heaps, Stacks, and Pointing   95

Heaps Versus Stacks 95

Pointers, References, and Arrays 97

Pointers Are Dangerous 105

Deleting from the Heap 106

Deleting Arrays 107

Summing Up 107

14   Testing   108

Why Storage from the Heap Makes Testing Critical 108

Making the Calculator More General with a
   "Little Language" 109

Debugging Without a Debugger 118

Summing Up 120

15 Structures and Types   121

Getting Organized 121

Declaring Enumerated Types 122

Declaring Structure Types 126

Structures on the Stack 126

Structures from the Heap 127

A Unidirectional Linked List with Structures for the Tape 128

Function Pointers and Callbacks 130

Summing Up 135

16 File I/O   136

Saving the Tape Between Sessions 136

Recalling the Tape 140

Replaying the Tape to Restore State 141

Summing Up 144

17 Classes: Structures with Functions   145

The Class as a Mini-Program 145

Classes Versus Instances 145

Constructors and Destructors 149

The Copy Constructor and When You Need It 154

Relaxing "Declare Before Use" Within Classes 155

Summing Up 156

18 Refactoring the Calculator with Classes   157

Moving Functions into Classes 157

Summing Up 161

19 Implementing the Calculator as Classes   163

Class Notation 163

The Private and Public Members of aRequest 165

Initialization 166
Internal State 168
Naming 171
Moving Function Content into Member Functions 172
The Object as Callback Structure 178
Who Allocates, Who Deletes, Who Uses, What's Shared 178
Summing Up 178

20 The Rest of the Calculator as Classes   179

Using a Standard C++ Library Class 179
The User Interface in an Object 184
The main.cpp 190
Summing Up 191

21 Function and Operator Overloading   192

Declaring Overloaded Member Functions in a Class 192
Overloaded Constructors 197
What Does It Mean to Overload an Operator? 197
Operator Overloading Can Be Dangerous 198
Overloading Assignment and the Copy Constructor 203
Summing Up 205

22 Inheritance   206

Declaring Inheritance 206
Referring to an Object as Its Class or Its Superclass 212
Overriding Functions 214
Protected Access 216
What Is virtual? 217
Virtual Constructors and Destructors 220
Virtual Member Functions 220
Calling the Superclass 220
Summing Up 221

23 Object Testing Using Inheritance   223

Writing Test Harnesses 223
Testing the Classes with Known Cases 224

Regression Testing 226
Summing Up 227

24   Abstract Classes, Multiple Inheritance, and Static Members   229

Creating Interfaces 229
Multiple Inheritance 237
Static Member Variables and Functions in Classes 240
Summing Up 245

25   Templates   247

Strengths and Weaknesses of Templates 247
Declaring and Using Templates 247
Summing Up 262

26   Performance: C++ Optimizations   263

Running Faster, Getting Smaller 263
Inlining 263
Incrementing and Decrementing 265
Templates Versus Generic Classes 266
Timing Your Code 266
Program/Data Structure Size 268
Summing Up 268

27   Wrapping Up   270

Things You Can Do to Enhance the Calculator 270
Lessons Learned 271

A   Operators   275

B   Operator Precedence   286

Index   289

About the Authors

Jesse Liberty is the author of more than a dozen programming books, including such international bestsellers as *Sams Teach Yourself C++ in 21 Days* and *Programming C#* (O'Reilly). Jesse is the president of Liberty Associates, Inc. (http://www.LibertyAssociates.com), where he provides .NET training, contract programming, and consulting. He is a former vice president of Citibank and a former distinguished software engineer and software architect for AT&T, Ziff Davis, PBS, and Xerox.

Mark Cashman is a multitalented information technology professional who has held positions ranging from software architect to head of information technology. His recent focus has been Internet eBusiness applications, where he has been responsible for enterprise-level technology investigation and adoption, enterprise application integration (EAI) framework design, and J2EE Web presentation architecture. He is a member of Borland TeamB, supporting C++Builder, is the author of sections of *C++Builder 5 Developer's Guide* (Sams) and of many articles for *C++Builder Developer's Journal*. His Web site, the Temporal Doorway (http://www.temporaldoorway.com), hosts programming tutorials in C++ and Java. He is currently developing the New England Trail Review (http://www.newenglandtrailreview.com), a taxonomy/content database-driven Web site for hiking trails in New England.

Dedication

This book is dedicated to the men and women working to keep us safe and free, and to the memory of September 11th.

—Jesse Liberty

Acknowledgments

I must first thank my family, who continue to support my writing and to put up with my insane schedule. I also want to thank the folks at Sams, especially Carol Ackerman, Matt Purcell, and Matt Wynalda. My thanks to Mark Cashman and Christopher McGee for helping to make this edition better than ever.

—Jesse Liberty

We Want to Hear from You!

As the reader of this book, *you* are our most important critic and commentator. We value your opinion and want to know what we're doing right, what we could do better, what areas you'd like to see us publish in, and any other words of wisdom you're willing to pass our way.

As an associate publisher for Sams, I welcome your comments. You can email or write me directly to let me know what you did or didn't like about this book—as well as what we can do to make our books better.

Please note that I cannot help you with technical problems related to the *topic* of this book. We do have a User Services group, however, where I will forward specific technical questions related to the book.

When you write, please be sure to include this book's title and author as well as your name, email address, and phone number. I will carefully review your comments and share them with the author and editors who worked on the book.

Email: feedback@samspublishing.com

Mail: Michael Stephens
Associate Publisher
Sams Publishing
800 East 96th Street
Indianapolis, IN 46240 USA

For more information about this book or another Sams title, visit our Web site at www.samspublishing.com. Type the ISBN (excluding hyphens) or the title of a book in the Search field to find the page you're looking for.

Introduction

When C++ has intrigued you, but you've never had the time to dig into its features and capabilities...

When your C++ skills are a little rusty from too much involvement elsewhere...

When you want to learn C++ programming, but don't want to buy a book heavier than your computer...

When there's something you want to know, but you don't want to wade through a reference manual to find it...

Sams Teach Yourself C++ in 10 Minutes is the book for you.

Read Lessons in 10 Minutes, Learn Quickly

You don't have the time to spend hours and hours reading. You need language knowledge and practical tips to help you make use of C++. And you need an approach that will let you see how real C++ programs are created and evolved to produce real results.

This guide doesn't try to teach you everything about C++ in huge chapters ripped from the reference manual. Instead, it focuses on the most important aspects of the language, basic and advanced, covering them in lessons designed to take around ten minutes each.

A Different Approach

If you want to learn how to write programs and you've never done it before, you'll want help in all aspects of programming. If you're a professional programmer, you'll want to know how C++ works in all phases of the software life cycle.

If either of these descriptions fits you, this book has been created with you in mind.

It follows the evolution of a single program from start to finish—letting you focus on the language, not on a new application for every example. It shows you how to build, enhance, fix, restructure, test, and optimize a program in C++. You get practical tips based on practical experience so that C++ can do the job for you.

What About C++?

This book shows you everything you need to know about C++, including its basic and advanced features, using clear explanations and diagrams to help you get the most out of every ten-minute lesson:

- Arithmetic
- Variables and constants
- Decision statements (`if` and `switch`) and logical expressions
- Loops (`do`, `while`, and `for`)
- Functions
- Input and output from users or from files
- Handling errors and exceptions
- Separate compilation
- Arrays, pointers, and references
- Function pointers
- Getting storage from the heap
- Data structures and user-defined types
- Classes and class members
- Function and operator overloading
- Inheritance and multiple inheritance

- Class polymorphism

- Templates

Once you have finished reading this book, whether you started as a beginner or as a seasoned programmer, you will be able to create and maintain professional-level programs in C++.

Conventions Used in This Book

Each lesson in this book explains a different aspect of C++ programming. The following icons will help you identify how particular pieces of information are used in this book:

Caution   This icon identifies areas where new users often run into trouble and offers practical solutions to those problems.

Note   The information in this box clarifies concepts and procedures in a straightforward manner.

Tip   Look here for ideas that cut corners and confusion.

Plain English   New or unfamiliar terms are defined in (you got it) "plain English."

Lesson 1
Getting Started

In this lesson, you will learn how to prepare, design, create, and modify programs written in C++.

The Mission

This book follows the life of a particular program from its creation through its maturity. Like many programs, it will start from a very simple concept, and will be enhanced in each lesson to offer more capabilities.

The purpose of this approach is to allow you to focus on the language and how it is used. Working on what is basically a single example throughout the entire book, you are free to concentrate on new features and how the C++ language supports them. Only a few parts of the example are created solely to demonstrate language features. Most additions and changes are realistic—driven by the program's purpose—just as your future programs will be.

You will learn several things in this book:

- The C++ language.

- The life cycle of software development.

- A process called evolutionary or adaptive development, which involves starting simply and gradually evolving a more complex program. This type of development is used frequently in professional programming.

The C++ Language

The C++ language was created as the next stage in the development of the C language. C, which was created by Brian Kernighan and Dennis Ritchie at Bell Labs between 1969 and 1973, was originally designed for programming low-level computer services such as operating systems (in Kernighan and Ritchie's case, Unix). It was meant to replace assembly language programming. Assembly programming led to programs that were hard to read and very difficult to create as separate units. C attained widespread acceptance and became the key language for Unix, and, eventually, Windows.

From its inception, C has been focused on producing high-performance programs, and so is C++.

C represents the *procedural* programming style of creating programs. Procedural programming creates programs that are a collection of functions or procedures, which operate on data to produce a result. Functions can call on other functions for services and assistance, which makes it possible to simplify problem solving using the "divide and conquer" strategy.

C is also a *strongly typed* language. This means that every item of data in C has a type and can only be used with other pieces of data in the ways that are defined by their types. *Weakly typed* languages, such as BASIC, either ignore or hide this important principle. Strong typing ensures that a program is reasonably correct, even before it is run for the first time.

Bjarne Stroustrup developed the C++ language in 1983 as an extension of C. C++ has most of the features of C. In fact, C++ programs can be written to look just like C programs—something you will do in the first part of this book. You can visit Stroustrup's Web site at http://www. research.att.com/~bs/C++.html. It is an excellent source for additional material.

C++ represents the *object-oriented* programming style. When you shift to writing object-oriented programs, you will see the similarities and differences between procedural and object-oriented programming.

Object-oriented programming views a program as a collection of classes that are used to produce objects. Each class contains a mix of data and functions. An object can call on objects of other classes for services and assistance. Because data is hidden away inside the class, object-oriented programs are safer and more easily modified than procedural programs (in which a change to the structure of data could affect functions all over the program).

Classes have member data and member functions, and because member data and member functions are almost exactly like their procedural counterparts, that's where we'll start.

Preparing to Program

The first question to ask when preparing to design any program is, "What is the problem I'm trying to solve?" Every program should have a clear, well-articulated goal, and you'll find that even the simplest version of the program in this book will have one.

C++, ANSI C++, Windows, and Other Areas of Confusion

Sams Teach Yourself C++ in 10 Minutes makes no assumptions about your computer. This book teaches ISO/ANSI Standard C++ (which from now on I'll just call Standard C++). The International Organization for Standardization (ISO), of which the American National Standards Institute (ANSI) is a member, is a standard-setting organization that publishes (among other things) documents that describe exactly how proper C++ programs will look and operate. You should be able to create such programs on any system.

You won't see anything in this book about windows, list boxes, graphics, and so forth. Collections of classes and functions (often called *libraries*) that work directly with your operating system (Windows, Unix, or Mac, for instance) provide these special features, but they are not part of the ISO/ANSI standard. Thus, the program in this book uses console input/output, which is simpler and is available on every system.

The program you will create can be easily adapted to use graphical user interface (GUI) features, so you can build on what you learn here to work with those libraries.

Your Compiler and Editor

For those unfamiliar with the term, a *compiler* is a program that takes a program written in a human-readable language (*source code*) and converts it into a file (the *executable*) that can be run on your computer using your operating system (Windows, Unix, or Mac, for instance). An *editor* is a program (such as the familiar Windows Notepad) that lets you type in the source code of your program and save it as a file. You will need at least one compiler and one editor to use this book.

This book assumes that you know how to use your editor to create, save, and modify text files and that you know how to use your compiler and any other necessary tools, such as a linker. Consult your operating system and compiler documentation for more on those topics.

The code in this book was compiled with Borland C++Builder 5 in strict ANSI mode. It has also been checked with Microsoft Visual Studio Version 6. There are numerous freeware and shareware compilers available to you, including one from Borland (http://www.borland.com), and the well-known gcc compiler (http://gcc.gnu.org). You can find information on available freeware/shareware compilers for C++ on the Web page for this book at http://www.samspublishing.com.

Getting Started with a New Project

You will need to make a directory for each piece of the program you create. Consult the documentation for your system if you are not familiar with how to do this. It is recommended that you create a top-level directory for this book, and then underneath that, create one for each lesson's example.

You can create your C++ source code files with your editor and save them in the directory for the corresponding lesson. Normally, source files have .cpp at the end (the file extension) to identify them as C++ code.

If you are using an *Integrated Development Environment (IDE)*, such as Borland's C++Builder or Microsoft's Visual C++, you can usually create a new project using File | New. In such environments, the program you are creating will need new console-type projects. You can save each project in the directory for the lesson, along with any of the source files that compose it. Please consult your IDE documentation for more details on this process.

The Development Cycle

If every program worked the first time you tried it, the complete development cycle would consist of writing the program, compiling the source code, and running it. Unfortunately, almost every program, no matter how simple, can and will have errors in it. Some errors will cause the compilation to fail, but some will only show up when you run the program.

In fact, every program's development goes through the following stages:

• **Analyze**—Decide what the program needs to do.

• **Design**—Determine how the program will do what it needs to do.

• **Edit**—Create source code based on the design.

• **Compile**—Use a compiler to turn the program into a file that your computer can run. The compiler will produce error messages if you have not written correct C++ "sentences," and you will need to understand these often-cryptic error messages and fix your code until you get a "clean compile."

• **Link**—Usually, the compiler will automatically link a clean-compiled program with any libraries it needs.

• **Test**—The compiler doesn't catch every error, so you must run the program, sometimes with specially planned input, and make sure that it does not do something wrong at runtime. Some runtime errors will just cause the operating system to stop the program, but others will produce the wrong results.

- **Debug**—Runtime errors require you to work with the program to find what is wrong. The problem is sometimes a design flaw, sometimes an incorrect use of a language feature, and sometimes an incorrect use of the operating system. Debuggers are special programs that help find these problems. If you don't have a debugger, you must include source code that will cause the program to tell you what it's doing at every stage.

Whatever type of bug you find, you must fix it, and that involves editing your source code, recompiling, relinking, and then rerunning the program until it is correct. You will engage in all of these activities in this book.

Evolving the Program

Once you complete a program, you will almost invariably find that you need it to do something additional or different. Users will want a new feature, or will find a runtime error you didn't discover in testing. Or you will be unhappy with the internal structure of the program and will want to refactor it to make it easier to understand or maintain.

A Simple Program

This simple program doesn't actually do anything, but the compiler doesn't care. You can compile and run this program with no problem.

Line Numbers in Code   The following listing contains line numbers. These numbers are for reference within the book. You should not type them in your editor. For example, in line 1 of Listing 1.1, you should enter

```
int main(int argc, char* argv[])
```

LISTING 1.1   main.cpp—an Empty Program

```
1: int main(int argc, char* argv[])
2: {
3:     return 0;
4: }
```

Make certain that you enter this exactly as shown (minus the line numbers). Pay careful attention to the punctuation. Line 3 ends with a semicolon; don't leave this off!

In C++, every character, including punctuation, is critical and must be entered correctly. In addition, C++ is case sensitive—return and Return, for instance, are not the same term.

Parts of the Program

This program consists of a single function called main. This function, which appears on line 1, has two parameters (inside the parentheses) and returns a number value (the starting int).

A *function* is a single group of code lines that perform a particular task. It has a heading at the top, with the function name as the second word and a body that starts with an opening brace ({) and ends with a closing brace (}). The closing brace optionally ends with a semicolon. More details about functions will be discussed in Lesson 7, "Functions."

main is a function that is required in all C++ programs. Your system provides the parameters it receives (called *arguments* for reasons beyond our interest in this lesson). These are

- int argc—The count of words in the line you typed to run the program.
- char* argv[]—The line you typed to run the program, broken into words.

The function has a *header* (line 1) and a *body* (lines 2–4). The *braces* on lines 2 and 4 show where the body starts and ends. Any set of lines with a brace before and after is called a *block* or *compound statement*. Line 3 is a *simple statement* that returns a number to the system when the program finishes—in this case, 0.

This program is a single .cpp file. Such a file is also called a *module*. Sometimes a module consists of two files—a header file (ending in .h) and a .cpp file. main.cpp doesn't need a header and never has one.

> The Return Value   The return value is always pro-
> vided but is no longer used very often (on Unix and
> DOS it may at times be used in batch files to signal
> success or failure of a program).

Compile-Time Errors

Compile-time errors in your program can be caused by a typing error or improper use of the language. Good compilers tell what you did wrong and point you to the exact place where you made the mistake. Occasionally, they can even suggest what you need to do to fix the error.

> Punctuation Errors   While modern compilers try to
> find the line on which your bug appears, the absence
> of a semicolon or closing brace can confuse the com-
> piler and you may find it pointing to a line that is oth-
> erwise fine. Beware of punctuation errors; they can be
> tricky to resolve.

You can test your compiler's reaction to an error by intentionally putting one into your program. If `main.cpp` runs smoothly, edit it now and remove the closing brace (line 4). Your program will look like Listing 1.2.

LISTING 1.2   Demonstration of a Compiler Error

```
1: int main(int argc, char* argv[])
2: {
3:     return 0;
```

Recompile your program, and you should see an error that looks similar to this:

```
[C++ Error] Main.cpp(3): E2134 Compound statement missing }
```

This error tells you the file and line number of the problem and what the problem is.

Sometimes the message can only get you to the general vicinity of the problem. For instance, leave off the first brace (line 2) instead of the last one (line 4) and you will get something like this:

```
[C++ Error] Main.cpp(3): E2141 Declaration syntax error
[C++ Error] Main.cpp(4): E2190 Unexpected }
```

Sometimes one error will cause another, as in this case. Usually, it is a good idea to fix the first few lines mentioned and then recompile.

If you can "think like a compiler," you will find error messages easier to understand. Compilers look at the source a word at a time and then a sentence at a time. They don't understand what the program means or what you intend for it to do.

Summing Up

In this lesson, you learned the history of C++ and the life cycle of a program. You created a simple C++ program, compiled it, and learned to interpret compiler error messages.

LESSON 2

Output to the Console— Standard Output

In this lesson, you will learn how to get your empty program to actually do something, how to work with libraries, and how to display program results.

Enhancing the Empty Program

Your first task is to add a line to the empty program so it won't be empty any longer. That line will display the program result.

Listing 2.1 shows the new version of main.cpp. A star before the line number indicates that the line is new. Do not enter the *, the line number, or the : in your code. These marks and numbers are only shown to help you to connect descriptions of the code with lines from the example.

LISTING 2.1   main.cpp Enhancements to Display a Result

```
 *1: #include <iostream>
 *2:
 *3: using namespace std;
 *4:
  5: int main(int argc, char* argv[])
  6: {
 *7:     // Without "using" statement, this would be std::cout
 *8:     cout << "Hi there!" << endl;  // "endl" = next line
  9:     return 0;
*10: }
```

Hi there!

This program displays the text "Hi there!" It does this by using a library of already-written program components called iostream. iostream has this name because it acts as if input and output are a stream of characters.

On line 1 the #include tells the compilers to include the header file iostream.h—the compiler is smart enough to know about the .h, so you don't have to put it in. This header file describes what components the library provides so that the compiler can recognize names such as cout.

Including the header file for iostream gives you the ability to use the iostream library. You can open the iostream.h file if you can find it on your system (usually in the include subdirectory of the directory where your compiler is installed). You will probably find its source code hard to understand. Fortunately, the compiler doesn't.

The iostream library includes the declaration of the standard output stream, referred to on line 8 as cout. It also includes the declaration of the stream inserter (<<) and a stream manipulator (endl).

The iostream library will generally be automatically linked with your code as part of the link phase. Check your compiler documentation to make sure.

The program's result will be displayed as text in the window or on the screen, depending on where you run the program.

The #include, Character by Character

The first character is the pound symbol (#), which is a signal to the *pre-processor*. The job of the preprocessor is to read through your source code looking for lines that begin with #, and when it finds one, to modify the code as requested by that command. This all happens before the compiler sees your code.

`include` is an instruction that says, "What follows is a filename. Find that file and read it in right here." The angle brackets around the filename tell the preprocessor, "Look in all the usual places for this file." If your compiler is set up correctly, the angle brackets will cause the preprocessor to look for the file `iostream.h` in the directory that holds all the header files for your compiler.

The effect of line 1 is to include the file `iostream.h` into this program as if you had typed that file into the code yourself.

Namespaces

Almost everything in a program has a name. When you start using libraries, there is always the chance that one library may have something in it that has the same name as something in another library. If that happens, the compiler can't tell which thing you meant to use. So C++ library programmers wrap their libraries in namespaces to keep their names separate.

Namespaces are a sort of container for names. Each namespace itself has a name that *qualifies* (is added to) any names in the code it holds. For instance, the namespace for `iostream` is named `std` (shorthand for "standard") and any name from that namespace is automatically qualified with `std`—as in `std::cout`.

The statement on line 3 tells the compiler, "If you see a name and you don't know what namespace it is from, assume it is from the `std` namespace."

If you leave this out, you will get the following message from the compiler:

```
[C++ Error] Main.cpp(8): E2451 Undefined symbol 'cout'
[C++ Error] Main.cpp(8): E2451 Undefined symbol 'endl'
```

This is because the compiler does not know where to look for `cout` and `endl`, since we never mention the namespace in which they can be found. We could cure this without the `using namespace` statement by changing line 8 to

```
std::cout << "Hi there!" << std::endl;
```

However, this isn't as readable, and because the things in the std namespace have been well known since before C++ had namespaces, the using namespace statement helps to keep it simple.

Comments

A *comment* is text you add to explain (to yourself or other programmers) why you have done something a particular way in your code. The comment does not make it through the compiler into the program file you actually run—it serves only as documentation.

Comments should not be used to explain everything. Use them to explain the design or why you chose to turn the design into this particular code.

There are two types of comments in C++. The double-slash (//) comment, which is referred to as a C++-style comment, tells the compiler to ignore everything that follows the slashes until the end of the line.

The C-style slash-star (/*) comment mark tells the compiler to ignore everything that follows until it finds a star-slash (*/) comment mark. These are less commonly used, except when a comment spans multiple lines.

Whitespace

Some lines in your program should be intentionally left blank. A blank line, called whitespace, makes it easier to read your program because it separates sections of code into related statements. Lines 2 and 4 are whitespace.

Sometimes a brace acts as whitespace, as on lines 6 and 10.

Functions

While main() is a function, it is an unusual one, because it is called automatically when you start your program. All other functions are called by your own code as the program runs.

A program is run line by line starting at the top of main, until another function is called. Control is then transferred to that function. When that function finishes, it returns control to the line after its call in main. If the function you call in turn calls another function, control flows in the same way—returning to the line in the first function that follows its call to the other function.

Even if a function is defined above main in the listing (you'll see this later), it is not performed before main. main always runs first.

Functions either return a value or return void (as in "the void of space"), meaning they return nothing. Note that main() always returns an int.

The cout Statement, Word by Word

The cout statement is what actually displays the program result on the screen or window. It is a special object from the iostream library.

The << symbol (two less-than signs) is an *inserter*, which takes whatever follows it and gives it to the cout object. Here you can see a little hint of what object-oriented programming is like.

What follows the inserter is a *literal* (as in "take this literally"). In this case, it is a *string* literal—a string of characters that consists of everything between the quotation marks.

The second inserter tacks an "end of line" (endl) on the end of the string literal display so that if anything further is displayed it will start on its own line. Different operating systems use different characters or combinations of characters to represent the end of a line, and endl lets you write a program that works on any operating system. The iostream library for your particular operating system knows which end-of-line character or characters to use.

Generally, every cout should have an endl, except, as you will see, when you use cout to get some input from a user.

Summing Up

In this lesson, you learned how to display the results from a program—in this case, a literal string. You used an important Standard C++ library (iostream) and identified the namespace to be searched for names not otherwise found. You saw some more compiler errors and learned how to use cout, the << inserter, and the endl manipulator to display a string of characters.

LESSON 3
Calculations

In this lesson, you will learn how to perform calculations, and how to display the results on the screen.

Performing and Displaying a Calculation

Now you are ready to move ahead and enhance the example you worked with in the last lesson. This time, you are replacing a line, not adding one. Have a look at Listing 3.1.

LISTING 3.1 The Example Performs a Calculation

```
 1: #include <iostream>
 2:
 3: using namespace std;
 4:
 5: int main(int argc, char* argv[])
 6: {
*7:     // Should print the number 6
*8:     cout << ((6/2)+3) << endl;
 9:     return 0;
10: }
```

OUTPUT This program displays the value 6, which is the result of calculating ((6/2)+3).

Expressions

((6/2)+3) is an example of an *expression*. In this case, the expression uses literal numbers, operators (/ and +), and parentheses.

Order of Evaluation

Every expression that uses operators must be interpreted by the compiler. In the simplest interpretation, the compiler could simply read the expression from left to right. If you leave out the parentheses, the expression looks like this:

```
6/2+3
```

If you perform this expression by hand, you get 6. But if the expression were

```
3+6/2
```

you would then get 4.5. This might not be what you want. Normally, multiplication and division are performed before addition and subtraction, so if you interpret

```
3+6/2
```

that way, you get 6 again.

C and C++ are operator-rich languages and have a complex set of rules that determine the *precedence* of operators. Higher precedence causes an operator and its *operands* (6 and 2 are the operands of / in the preceding expression) to be evaluated before any operator and operands with lower precedence (an operator and its operands are sometimes called *subexpressions*).

Programmers often don't do well at remembering these rules. If you have any doubt, use parentheses. In fact, even if you *don't* have any doubt, parentheses are a good idea.

Parentheses guarantee a specific precedence. Subexpressions in parentheses are evaluated at a higher precedence than any of the mathematical operators. For instance

```
3+(6/2)
```

will guarantee that 6 is divided by 2 before 3 is added to that result.

You can find more information on C++ operators and their normal precedence in Appendix B, "Operator Precedence."

Nesting Parentheses

With complex expressions, you might need to *nest* parentheses (to put a subexpression inside another subexpression). For example:

```
4*(3+(6/2))
```

This complicated expression should be read from the inside out. First, divide 6 by 2. Then add 3 to that result. Then multiply the updated result by 4.

Because C++ doesn't require an expression to be written on a single line, you can make this more understandable by using the parentheses as if they were braces:

```
4*
(
    3+
    (6/2)
)
```

This makes it easier to be sure that every opening parenthesis has a closing parenthesis (thus avoiding a common programming mistake).

Expressions in cout

`iostream` can display the result of a complex expression just as easily as it can display a simple string literal. In the example program, an expression is placed in the `cout` statement, and the number 6 is written on the screen as simply as "Hi there!" was in Lesson 2.

This works because the compiler causes the expression to be evaluated before providing its result to the `cout` statement.

Using an Input Stream

If you are using an Integrated Development Environment (IDE), such as Borland's C++Builder or Microsoft's Visual C++, you may find that running the example creates a window where the result (if any) is displayed, and the window almost instantly disappears when the program stops

running. If that happens, you'll need to make the program pause before it
ends to see whether the output is what you expect.

Even if you are running your programs directly from the command line of
a DOS or shell window, you will find the following code interesting, as it
lets the program get information from the user.

```
 1: #include <iostream>
 2:
 3: using namespace std;
 4:
 5: int main(int argc, char* argv[])
 6: {
 7:    cout << ((6/2)+3) << endl;
*8:
*9:    // Note: You must type something before the Enter key
*10:   char StopCharacter;
*11:   cout << endl << "Press a key and \"Enter\": ";
*12:   cin >> StopCharacter;
*13:
 14:   return 0;
 15:}
```

ANALYSIS   Lines 8–13 are new. Lines 8 and 13 are whitespace and line
9 is a comment. Lines 10–12 are the ones that count.

Line 10 declares a variable. This variable is a place to keep the single
character that the user must type to end the pause. You can tell what input
is expected because of the word char, which identifies what type of variable this is. Since C++ requires every variable to have a name, this one is
called StopCharacter.

Line 11 contains a string. This string will be displayed as follows:

OUTPUT   Press a key and "Enter":

Note that the backslashes (\) in line 11 allow you to use quotation marks
inside a string literal. Without a \, the compiler sees a quote and assumes
that it has reached the end of the string literal. Try taking it out and see
what happens. You will probably get an error message when you try to
compile the program.

Line 12 waits for a single character from the user (this is the pause) and
puts it in StopCharacter. The cin standard input stream from <iostream>

is used for this purpose. Here, you can see the use of the >> operator, which is called the *extractor*. The extractor points the opposite direction from the inserter. Through its direction it shows that information is coming from `cin` and is being put in the variable.

Now the program runs, and prints 6. Then it prints the string `Press a key` and `"Enter"`: (this kind request for input is often called a *prompt*). It waits for the user to press a letter, number, or punctuation key on the keyboard followed by the Enter key. When that happens, the program returns 0 and stops.

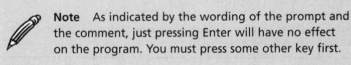

> **Note**   As indicated by the wording of the prompt and the comment, just pressing Enter will have no effect on the program. You must press some other key first.

Variables

Earlier, you saw how almost everything in a program has a name. Of course, literals are an exception to this rule. They are what they are and they have no name.

Variables let you give a name to a value. Actually, you are naming a place to keep that data in the computer's memory.

When you define a variable in C++, you must tell the compiler not only what its name is, but also what kind of information it will hold: a number, a character (such as `char StopCharacter`), or something else. This is called a variable's *type*. You may recall that C++ is said to be a strongly typed language, and identifying the type of a variable is part of what makes strong typing work.

The type of the variable tells the compiler, among other things, how much room to set aside in memory to hold the variable's value. It also lets the compiler make sure that the variable is used appropriately (for instance, it will produce an error message if you try to divide a number by a character).

The smallest unit of memory used for a variable is called a *byte*.

Size of Storage

In most cases, a character is one byte in size, but for international applications, a character may require more than one byte.

> **The ASCII Character Set**   Variables of type char typically contain values from the ASCII character set. This is a set of 256 characters standardized for use on computers. ASCII is an acronym for American Standard Code for Information Interchange. Nearly every computer operating system supports ASCII. However, ASCII cannot represent some large character sets such as Japanese, which require characters more than one byte in size (multibyte characters) due to the large size of their alphabet. A type called wchar_t is often used for such characters.

A short int is 2 bytes on most computers, a long int is usually 4 bytes, and an int (without the keyword short or long) can be 2 or 4 bytes. If you are running Windows 95, Windows 98, or Windows NT, your int is likely to be 4 bytes in size, but you should rarely (and then only carefully) depend on this.

Using int Variables and Constants

A variable allows the program to perform its calculation outside of the cout statement.

```
 1: #include <iostream>
 2:
 3: using namespace std;
 4:
 5: int main(int argc, char* argv[])
 6: {
*7:     const int Dividend = 6;
*8:     const int Divisor = 2;
*9:
*10:    int Result = (Dividend/Divisor);
```

```
*11:    Result = Result + 3;// Result is now its old value+3=6
*12:
*13:    cout << Result << endl;
 14:
 15:    // Note: You must type something before the Enter key
 16:    char StopCharacter;
 17:    cout << endl << "Press a key and \"Enter\": ";
 18:    cin >> StopCharacter;
 19:
 20:    return 0;
 21: }
```

ANALYSIS   Lines 7–13 have been changed.

Lines 7 and 8 *declare* variables named Dividend and Divisor and set their values to 6 and 3, respectively. The = is called the *assignment operator* and puts the value on the right-hand side into the variable on the left-hand side. These variables are declared as type int, which is a number with no decimal places.

Although these are technically variables, because they have names, the use of the word const on these variable declarations makes it clear to the compiler that the program is not allowed to change the content of these variables in any way (unlike, for instance, the variable StopCharacter, which stores whatever character the user types in). Declarations with const are often called *constants* (mathematically inclined readers will recall that *pi* is the name of the constant whose value is 3.14159).

Line 10 declares a variable and assigns the result of part of an expression to the variable. It uses the names of the constants on lines 7 and 8 in the expression, so the value in Result depends on the content of those constants.

Line 11 is perhaps the hardest one for non-programmers. Remember that the variable is a named location in memory and that its content can change over time. Line 11 says, "Add the current content of Result and the number 3 together and put the calculated value into the location named by Result, wiping out what used to be there."

OUTPUT   The output of this example is still 6. This shows that you can change the *implementation* of a design (that is, the code you have written to accomplish a task), and still produce the same result.

Therefore, it is possible to alter a program to make it more readable or maintainable.

Types of Variables and Valid Names

Integers come in two varieties: `signed` and `unsigned`. The idea here is that sometimes you need negative numbers, and sometimes you don't. Integers (`short` and `long`) that aren't labeled `unsigned` are assumed to be `signed`. `signed` integers are either negative or positive. `unsigned` integers are always positive.

Use `int` for Number Variables   For most programs, most of the time, you can simply declare your simple number variables as `ints`—these are signed integers.

Non-Integer Variable Types

Several variable types are built into C++. They can be conveniently divided into integer variables (the type discussed so far), character variables (usually `char`), and floating-point variables (`float` and `double`).

Floating-Point Variables   Floating-point variables can have fractional values and decimal points, unlike integers.

The types of variables used in C++ programs are described in Table 3.1. This table shows the variable types, how much room they typically take in memory, and what ranges of values can be stored in these variables. The variable type determines the values that can be stored, so check your output from Listing 3.1.

Note that the *e* in 3.4e38 (the number at the high end of the range of values for `float`) means "times ten to the power of," so the expression

should be read "3.4 times ten to the 38th power," which is
340,000,000,000,000,000,000,000,000,000,000,000,000.

TABLE 3.1   Variable Types

Type	Size	Values
unsigned short int	2 bytes	0 to 65,535
short int	2 bytes	−32,768 to 32,767
unsigned long int	4 bytes	0 to 4,294,967,295
long int	4 bytes	−2,147,483,648 to 2,147,483,647
char	1 byte	256 character values
bool	1 byte	true or false
float	4 bytes	1.2e−38 to 3.4e38
double	8 bytes	2.2e−308 to 1.8e308

Strings

String variables are a special case. They are called arrays and will be discussed in more detail later.

Case Sensitivity

C++ is *case sensitive*. This means that words with different combinations of uppercase and lowercase letters are considered different words. A variable named age is not the same variable as Age or AGE.

 Caution   This is the most common error made by programmers when reading or writing C++. Be careful.

Keywords

Some words are reserved by C++, and you may not use them as variable names. These are keywords used by the compiler to understand your program. Keywords include `if`, `while`, `for`, and `main`. Your compiler manual should provide a complete list, but generally, any reasonable name for a variable is almost certainly not a keyword. See the inside back cover of this book for a list of some C++ keywords.

Summing Up

In this lesson, you saw how to use literals and how to declare and define variables and constants. You also saw how to assign values to these variables and constants, and what values and names are valid. And you saw how to get input from the user, a subject that will be covered in greater detail in the next lesson.

LESSON 4
Numeric Input

In this lesson, you'll see how to get some input for the calculator and look at what happens when the input is something other than a number.

Numeric Input

A program that performs calculations on predefined numbers is a good start, but most programs need to perform operations on data from the outside world. So let's extend the example again as shown in Listing 4.1.

LISTING 4.1   Getting Numeric Input from the User

```
 1: #include <iostream>
 2:
 3: using namespace std;
 4:
 5: int main(int argc, char* argv[])
 6: {
*7:     int Dividend = 1;
*8:     cout << "Dividend: ";
*9:     cin >> Dividend;
*10:
*11:    int Divisor = 1;
*12:    cout << "Divisor: ";
*13:    cin >> Divisor;
 14:
 15:    int Result = (Dividend/Divisor);
 16:    cout << Result << endl;
 17:
 18:    // Note: You must type something before the Enter key
 19:    char StopCharacter;
*20:    cout << endl << "Press a key and \"Enter\": ";
*21:    cin >> StopCharacter;
 22:
 23:    return 0;
 24: }
```

ANALYSIS The interesting part here is in lines 7–13. The constants have been replaced with input into variables, similar to the input requested on lines 20 and 21 (which consist of code from the previous lesson). The program now only does division, which makes it simpler and more general.

Line 7 creates the `Dividend`, now a variable. The Dividend is set initially (or *initialized*) to a value of 1. Even though the program is getting input from the user to set these variables, it is always a good idea to make sure variables are set to some sensible initial value—this is often referred to as *defensive programming*.

Line 8 uses the `cout` standard output stream to display a prompt to the user.

Line 9 gets a number from the standard input stream and puts it into the `Dividend` variable.

Lines 11–13 repeat the same set of actions for the `Divisor` variable.

Here's what you get when you test:

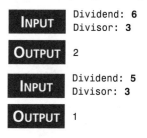

INPUT
```
Dividend: 6
Divisor: 3
```

OUTPUT `2`

INPUT
```
Dividend: 5
Divisor: 3
```

OUTPUT `1`

What's the Problem?

While the first answer makes sense, the second one doesn't. If you use a regular calculator, you'll find that 5/3 = 1.6666667. So why does the program produce 1?

The answer is fairly simple, though annoying. The program is using the `int` type, which means that the division used is *integer division*. Integer division just clips off any digits to the right of the decimal point. This is usually called *truncation*.

You can make the calculator more accurate by using the float type, which allows digits to the right of the decimal point—unlike the int type.

LISTING 4.2   Getting Numeric Input from the User as float

```
 1: #include <iostream>
 2:
 3: using namespace std;
 4:
 5: int main(int argc, char* argv[])
 6: {
*7:     float Dividend = 1;
 8:       cout << "Dividend: ";
 9:       cin >> Dividend;
10:
*11:    float Divisor = 1;
12:      cout << "Divisor: ";
13:      cin >> Divisor;
14:
*15:    float Result = (Dividend/Divisor);
16:      cout << Result << endl;
17:
18:      // Note: You must type something before the Enter key
19:      char StopCharacter;
20:      cout << endl << "Press a key and \"Enter\": ";
21:      cin >> StopCharacter;
22:
23:      return 0;
24: }
```

Only lines 7, 11, and 15 are different from Listing 4.1, and the only change is that the variable type keyword is float instead of int.

Now run the tests again. This is called *regression testing* and helps to make sure that the changes have done the job.

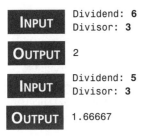

INPUT	Dividend: **6** Divisor: **3**
OUTPUT	2
INPUT	Dividend: **5** Divisor: **3**
OUTPUT	1.66667

Now the calculator works (at least for these specific tests).

But all of the tests so far have used values that ought to work. Such tests are called *within-bounds* tests. They are important, but are not sufficient. You also need to use *out-of-bounds* tests.

In order to perform such testing, provide input that is clearly outside the normal range for the program—in this case, a letter rather than a number.

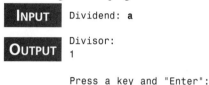

```
INPUT     Dividend: a

          Divisor:
OUTPUT    1

          Press a key and "Enter":
```

With this input, the program does not wait for the user to input a divisor. It displays a wrong answer and doesn't wait for the user input to the Press a key and "Enter": prompt. This is certainly not what you would expect. The next step will be to investigate the problem and determine exactly what is happening.

What Went Wrong?

This is one of the most feared problems a programmer must face. The program did something terribly wrong—so wrong that it behaved completely unexpectedly. How can you find out what happened?

In this case, you can use cout statements to find out where the program "died." These statements provide a status report at the beginning of each step in the program. When a status report is not provided, you will know that the program stopped in the code just before that step.

To let these *debugging statements* show what is happening at each stage, the program will pause after each status report and require the user to enter a character.

Listing 4.3 shows the example with these debugging statements.

LISTING 4.3   Example with Debugging Statements

```
1: #include <iostream>
2:
```

LISTING 4.3   Continued

```
 3: using namespace std;
 4:
 5: int main(int argc, char* argv[])
 6: {
 7:     char DebugGoOn;
 8:     cout << "Dividend..." << endl;
 9:     cin >> DebugGoOn;
10:
11:     float Dividend = 1;
12:     cout << "Dividend: ";
13:     cin >> Dividend;
14:
15:     cout << "Divisor..." << endl;
16:     cin >> DebugGoOn;
17:
18:     float Divisor = 1;
19:     cout << "Divisor: ";
20:     cin >> Divisor;
21:
22:     cout << "Calculating..." << endl;
23:     cin >> DebugGoOn;
24:
25:     float Result = (Dividend/Divisor);
26:     cout << Result << endl;
27:
28:     cout << "Calculation done." << endl;
29:     cin >> DebugGoOn;
30:
31:     // Note: You must type something before the Enter key
32:     char StopCharacter;
33:     cout << endl << "Press a key and \"Enter\": ";
34:     cin >> StopCharacter;
35:
36:     return 0;
37: }
```

OUTPUT   And here's the result:

```
Dividend...
                    .
Dividend: a
Divisor...
Divisor: Calculating...
```

```
1
Calculation done.

Press some key and "Enter" to terminate the program:
```

This confirms that the program does not actually "die," but it also suggests that getting a bad character in expected numeric input makes the input stream unusable for the rest of the program's run.

> **Note**   Debugging a program with `cout` and `cin` is notoriously error-prone itself, because adding and removing the debugging statements can damage the source code in unexpected ways should the programmer make an error. If you have a real debugger (for instance, as part of an Integrated Development Environment), use it instead.

What can you do to correct the problem? The next lesson will take up that question.

Summing Up

In this lesson, you learned how to get input from the user into a numeric variable. You learned about the pitfalls of integer arithmetic and saw how terrible errors can happen when a program gets input from the user. In the next lesson you will learn how to recover from such errors.

LESSON 5

if Statements and Program Decisions

In this lesson, you will learn how to use the if *statement. You will see how to handle errors, use Boolean logic and will extend our example to enable it to recover from bad input.*

Dealing with a Failed Input Stream

It took two days of research and a lot of thinking to come up with the sample code in Listing 5.1. But, since you only have 10 minutes, let's dive right into it.

LISTING 5.1 Getting Numeric Input and Recovering from an Error

```
 1:  #include <iostream>
 2:
 3:  using namespace std;
 4:
 5:  int main(int argc, char* argv[])
 6:  {
*7:     int ReturnCode = 0;
 8:
 9:     float Dividend = 0;
10:     cout << "Dividend: ";
11:     cin >> Dividend;
12:
*13:    if (!cin.fail()) // Dividend is a number
*14:    {
15:        float Divisor = 1;
```

LISTING 5.1 Continued

```
16:          cout << "Divisor: ";
17:          cin >> Divisor;
18:
19:          float Result = (Dividend/Divisor);
20:          cout << Result << endl;
*21:     }
*22:     else // Dividend is not a number
*23:     {
*24:          cerr << "Input error, not a number?" << endl;
*25:
*26:          cin.clear(); // Reset the input failure indicators
*27:          // Eat the bad input so we can pause the program
*28:          char BadInput[5]; // Up to 5 characters
*29:          cin >> BadInput;
*30:
*31:          ReturnCode = 1;
*32:     };
33:
34:      // Note: You must type something before the Enter key
35:      char StopCharacter;
36:      cout << endl << "Press a key and \"Enter\": ";
37:      cin >> StopCharacter;
38:
*39:     return ReturnCode;
40: }
```

The key to this code is in line 13—the if statement.

The if Statement

The if statement in line 13 is used to control which portion of the code will be run next. As discussed in an earlier lesson, a program normally starts running at the top of the main function and ends at the bottom, only deviating from this order when calling a function to perform some service.

However, a program that performs the same code on every run is not as flexible as code that runs differently in different circumstances.

The if statement is the key to that ability. It uses a bool expression to make its decision.

How to Decide

The 1998 ISO/ANSI standard introduced a special type called `bool` (named for George Boole, the famed developer of Boolean algebra, which is the basis for all program decision-making).

This new type has two possible values, `false` and `true`. You can think of these as 0 and 1.

Every expression can be evaluated for its truth or falsity. Expressions that evaluate mathematically to zero have a value of `false`; all others have a value of `true`.

The `if` statement relies on the `bool` type. A `true` value causes the `if` statement to perform one set of statements; `false` causes it to follow another path.

The `if` statement, then, has the following format:

```
if (/* bool expression */)
{
    // if true, this part of the code runs
}
else
{
    // if false, this part of the code runs
};
```

In line 13 of the example, the `if` statement is using (also called *testing*) the `bool` expression `!cin.fail()`. This expression is an operator (`!`) applied to a call of the `cin` object's function `fail()`. The function returns `true` when there has been an error in the input stream.

Because the code that runs when the input is good should be the main thrust of the program source, the expression uses a special operator on the function result—the `!` operator (sometimes called the *bang operator* or the *not operator*). The bang operator takes a `true` result and makes it `false` or takes a `false` result and makes it `true`.

The bang operator is what is called a *prefix unary operator*, which is to say it must appear before its operand (it is a prefix), and it has only one operand (it is unary). This is different from the addition operator (+), which is an example of an *infix operator*—one that goes between two operands.

The bang operator is often read as "not," so the !cin.bad() expression would be read as "not cin bad."

To improve the readability of the if statement, the code in each of the blocks has been indented. You'll also notice the use of braces to enclose the code in each of the blocks.

Error Recovery

You'll notice that the error message is not sent to cout, but to a new stream called cerr. This is the standard error stream, and while it is almost always the same as the standard output stream—that is, error messages appear on the same screen or window—on occasion it is different. At any rate, it is always the right place to send error messages.

Lines 24–28 recover from the error by clearing the state of the stream on line 26, and then "eating" the characters that are waiting in the output stream. If you don't do this, even with the stream state set to "not bad," the next cin request will get the bad characters entered (often called *pending characters*) and will not wait for the user when it should pause before ending the run.

The declaration char BadInput[5] in line 28 creates space for up to five characters, which the next cin attempts to get from the input stream. Failure to get all five does not constitute an error condition, so this section of the code can safely eat as many as five characters of bad input, which will allow the normal pre-stop pause to work properly.

In addition, main() sets the ReturnCode variable to 1, just in case a shell script or batch file wants to know that the program encountered an error. It doesn't just return a literal any more—now it returns the content of the variable ReturnCode.

This example does not yet handle the case when the input for the Divisor is wrong. Listing 5.2 contains the code that does so.

LISTING 5.2   Getting Numeric Input and Recovering from an Error on Input of Either Dividend or Divisor

```
1: #include <iostream>
2:
3: using namespace std;
4:
5: int main(int argc, char* argv[])
6: {
7:     int ReturnCode = 0;
8:
9:     float Dividend = 0;
10:    cout << "Dividend: ";
11:    cin >> Dividend;
12:
13:    if (!cin.fail()) // Dividend is a number
14:    {
15:        float Divisor = 1;
16:        cout << "Divisor: ";
17:        cin >> Divisor;
18:
19:        if (!cin.fail()) // Divisor is a number
20:        {
21:            float Result = (Dividend/Divisor);
22:            cout << Result << endl;
23:        }
24:        else // Divisor is not a number
25:        {
26:            cerr << "Input error, not a number?" << endl;
27:
28:            cin.clear(); // Reset the input failure bits
29:            // Eat the bad input so we can pause the program
30:            char BadInput[5]; // Up to 5 characters
31:            cin >> BadInput;
32:
33:            ReturnCode = 1;
34:        };
35:    }
36:    else // Dividend is not a number
37:    {
38:        cerr << "Input error, not a number?" << endl;
39:
40:        cin.clear(); // Reset the input failure indicators
41:        // Eat the bad input so we can pause the program
```

LISTING 5.2   Continued

```
42:        char BadInput[5];  // Up to 5 characters
43:        cin >> BadInput;
44:
45:        ReturnCode = 1;
46:    }
47:
48:    // Note: You must type something before the Enter key
49:    char StopCharacter;
50:    cout << endl << "Press a key and \"Enter\": ";
51:    cin >> StopCharacter;
52:
53:    return ReturnCode;
54: }
```

The check for an error in the Divisor is inside the true block of the *outer* if statement that checked for an error in getting the Dividend. This "if-within-if" is called a *nested* if *statement*. The blocks for the inner if statement are indented further to keep things as readable as possible.

> **Note** It is easy to use many levels of nested if statements and produce an unreadable program that even indentation cannot improve. Later lessons will show how to use functions to overcome this potential problem.
>
> Also note that the C++ if statement only has an else keyword—there is no then keyword, as there is in some languages such as Pascal. Despite this, the block performed when the if statement bool expression is true may be referred to as a then block.

Summing Up

In this lesson, you saw the use of the if statement to detect the occurrence of an input error. You also saw how to reset the stream and recover from the error.

LESSON 6
Exception Handling

In this lesson, you will learn how to use the try/catch *statement to perform error handling.*

Exception Handling—A Better Way

If you take a high-level look at the example you've been building, you can see that error-handling code now dominates it. While this is not unusual for professional programs, it is inconvenient to have error-handling code interlaced with normal processing code. You might also notice that the two else blocks contain essentially the same error-handling code.

Earlier forms of the example took some steps to separate the error and non-error code by using the bang operator to keep the normal processing code near the top and error-processing code near the bottom.

However, C++ offers a better way to deal with errors, called exception handling. Under exception handling, code that encounters an error throws an exception, which is caught by a special section of exception-handling code.

Exceptions are handled using the try/catch statement:

```
try
{
    // Code for normal, non-error processing
}
catch (/* Exception variable declaration */)
{
    // Code to handle the error
};
```

Listing 6.1 shows how the example looks when it uses exception handling.

LISTING 6.1 Exception Handling to Catch Bad Input

```
 1: #include <iostream>
 2:
 3: using namespace std;
 4:
 5: int main(int argc, char* argv[])
 6: {
 7:     // Prepare to have failed input throw an exception
*8:     cin.exceptions(cin.failbit);
 9:
10:     int ReturnCode = 0;
11:
*12:     try // Normal processing section
*13:     {
14:         float Dividend = 0;
15:         cout << "Dividend: ";
16:         cin >> Dividend;
17:
18:         float Divisor = 1;
19:         cout << "Divisor: ";
20:         cin >> Divisor;
21:
22:         float Result = (Dividend/Divisor);
23:
24:         cout << Result << endl;
25:     }
*26:     catch (...) // Error handling section
*27:     {
*28:         cerr <<
*29:             "Input error, not a number?" <<
*30:             endl;
31:
32:         cin.clear(); // Clear the error state
33:
34:         // Eat the bad input so we can pause the program
35:         char BadInput[5]; // Up to 5 characters
36:         cin >> BadInput;
37:
38:         ReturnCode = 1;
39:     };
40:
```

LISTING 6.1 Continued

```
41:     // Note: You must type something before the Enter key
42:     char StopCharacter;
43:     cout << endl << "Press a key and \"Enter\": ";
44:     cin >> StopCharacter;
45:
46:     return ReturnCode;
47: }
```

Running this code produces the following:

OUTPUT

```
Dividend: a
Input error - input may not have been a number
     .

Press some key and "Enter" to terminate the program:.
```

ANALYSIS Line 8 prepares cin to throw an exception when an error occurs. This is specific to the iostream library and requires the use of a special constant to identify the error condition that will provoke an exception.

Lines 12 and 13 mark the start of the code that might throw an exception. If any of these lines or any functions they call throw an exception, the subsequent lines will be skipped and the exception will be caught at line 26.

Where can you find the things you need to know to catch an exception? Libraries are the source of most exceptions and the exceptions they throw are generally documented in the same places as the library classes or library functions that throw them. iostream exceptions are not especially well documented and uncovering their names and causes required some Internet research.

Why Use Exceptions?

Exceptions may seem somewhat more technical than `if` statements, but they are the preferred way to handle errors in C++. Whereas older libraries used to report errors with "error codes," most modern libraries throw exceptions instead.

In addition, exception handling cleans up the code. While error handling is an important component of any real program, programmers generally want to read normal processing code and error-handling code separately, because that makes each of them easier to understand. Exceptions provide the best way to accomplish this.

Summing Up

In this lesson, you saw the use of the `try/catch` statement to detect the occurrence of an input error. `try/catch` makes the code cleaner and easier to read. It also avoids duplication of error-handling code.

LESSON 7
Functions

In this lesson, you will learn to split your program into multiple functions so that each segment of code can be simplified.

What Is a Function?

When people talk about C++, they mention objects first. Yet objects rely on functions to get their work done. A *function* is, in effect, a subprogram that can act on data and return a value. Every C++ program has at least one function—main(). When your program starts, main() is called automatically. main() might call other functions, some of which might call still others.

Each function has its own name, and when that name is encountered, the execution of the program branches to the body of that function. This process is known as *calling* the function. When the function completes all of its code, it returns, and execution resumes on the next line of the calling function. This flow is illustrated in Figure 7.1.

A well-designed function will perform a specific task. That means it does one thing and then returns.

Complicated tasks should be broken down into multiple functions, and then each can be called in turn. This makes your code easier to understand and easier to maintain.

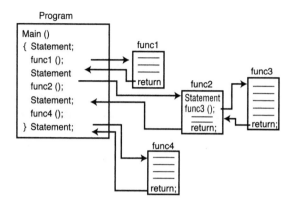

FIGURE 7.1 When a program calls a function, execution switches to the function and then resumes at the line after the function call.

Defining Functions

Before you can use a function, you must first define the function header and then the function body.

A function header definition consists of the function's return type, name, and argument list. Figure 7.2 illustrates the parts of the function header.

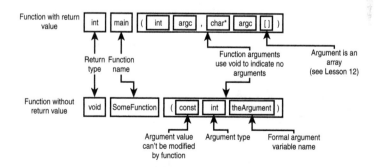

FIGURE 7.2 Parts of a function header.

> **Parameters or Arguments?**   The values passed to a function are its arguments. Arguments come in two flavors: formal (in the function header) and actual (in the function call). Formal arguments are also called parameters. Actual arguments are the values passed in during a call to the function. Most programmers use the terms *parameter* and *argument* interchangeably, but we will try to remain consistent, using *argument* as the term of choice.

The body of the function is a set of statements enclosed in braces. Figure 7.3 shows the header and body of a function.

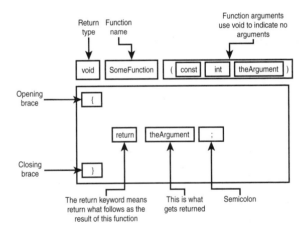

FIGURE 7.3   The header and body of a function.

Breaking the Example into Functions

The program is getting a bit long by now. Even with the use of exception handling to reduce the amount of error code, it is getting a little hard to follow. So you can split it into functions, each of which is a smaller and more understandable piece of largely self-contained code with a name that indicates its purpose. Listing 7.1 shows what the program looks like when you do this.

LISTING 7.1   The Example as Functions

```
 1: #include <iostream>
 2:
 3: using namespace std;
 4:
 5: void Initialize(void) // No return value, no arguments
 6: {
 7:     cin.exceptions(cin.failbit);
 8: }
 9:
10: float GetDividend(void) // Returns dividend, a float
11: {
12:     float Dividend = 0;
13:
14:     cout << "Dividend: ";
15:     cin >> Dividend;
16:
17:     return Dividend; // Returns a copy of Dividend
18: }
19:
20: float GetDivisor(void) // Returns the divisor
21: {
22:     float Divisor = 1;
23:
24:     cout << "Divisor: ";
25:     cin >> Divisor;
26:
27:     return Divisor;
28: }
29:
30: float Divide
        ➥(const float theDividend,const float theDivisor)
        ➥// Takes unmodifiable (const) arguments, returns
        ➥float
31: {
32:     return (theDividend/theDivisor);
            ➥// Returns the result of the calculation
33: }
34:
```

LISTING 7.1 Continued

```
35: int HandleNotANumberError(void) // Returns the error code
36: {
37:     cerr <<
38:         "Input error - input may not have been a number."
39:         <<endl;
40:
41:     cin.clear(); // Clear the error state from the stream
42:
43:     // Eat the bad input so we can pause the program
44:     char BadInput[5];
45:     cin >> BadInput;
46:
47:     return 1; // An error occurred
48: }
49:
50: void PauseForUserAcknowledgement(void)
51: {
52:     // Note: You must type something before the Enter key
53:     char StopCharacter;
54:     cout << endl << "Press a key and \"Enter\": ";
55:     cin >> StopCharacter;
56: }
57:
58: int main(int argc, char* argv[])
59: {
60:     Initialize(); // Call the function
61:
62:     int ReturnCode = 0;
63:
64:     try
65:     {
66:         float Dividend = GetDividend();
67:         float Divisor = GetDivisor();
68:
69:         cout << Divide(Dividend,Divisor) << endl;
70:     }
71:     catch (...)
72:     {
73:         ReturnCode = HandleNotANumberError();
74:     };
75:
76:     PauseForUserAcknowledgement();
77:     return ReturnCode;
78: }
```

ANALYSIS   First look at the program's `main()` function (lines 58–78). Almost all of the code has been removed from it and replaced with calls to other functions, which will be discussed in the following sections.

A Function with No Arguments or Return Value

Line 60 calls a function to initialize the program—in this case, this simply tells `cin` what error conditions will cause the exception, just as in the previous version.

```
void Initialize(void) // No return value, no arguments
{
    cin.exceptions(cin.failbit);
}
```

This is a simple function that takes no arguments and returns no value. Compare this with the `main()` function, which does have arguments and does return a value.

Remember that `void` (as in "the void of space") means "nothing." So the function returns nothing and gets nothing as an argument.

A Function with No Arguments but with Local Variables and a Return Value

Line 66 prompts the user and gets the `Dividend`.

Here is the function:

```
float GetDividend(void) // Returns the dividend (an integer)
{
    float Dividend = 0;

    cout << "Dividend: ";
    cin >> Dividend;

    return Dividend; // Returns a copy of Dividend
}
```

This function takes no arguments but does return a value. Notice the local variable `Dividend`, which is used so that the `cin` statement has somewhere to put the input. This variable is created when the function is entered and disappears when the function is finished. The return statement puts a copy of the content of the variable in a nameless temporary location from which the code in main() will be able to pick it up. Also notice that the names of the local variables in GetDividend() and in main() are the same. Because these two functions are independent, this is allowed and does not interfere with the values in either variable.

A Function with Arguments and a Return Value

Line 69 calls the Divide function, passing the dividend and divisor. The function returns the result of the division. Notice that it does not use a local variable, though it could.

```
float Divide
    ➥(float theDividend,float theDivisor)
        ➥// Takes arguments, returns integer
{
    return (theDividend/theDivisor);
}
```

This function takes two arguments. Arguments are called *formal* when they are in the function head. They only serve as placeholders for whatever actual literal, expression, or other value is provided to the function when it is called.

To reinforce this idea, the program follows a specific convention for naming formal arguments—they start with a lowercase "the" (theDividend, theDivisor). This makes it easy to distinguish between arguments and local variables when reading the code. Because arguments represent incoming data for the function, they are the most critical potential source of problems and you want to be able to quickly and easily see where they are being used.

Convention   A somewhat arbitrary decision about a consistent way to do something. There are naming conventions for variables and structuring conventions for programs.

A Function Call with Arguments That Are Themselves Function Calls

An alternative form for Line 69 is

```
cout << Divide(GetDividend(),GetDivisor()) << endl;
```

Here again, you can see the effects of precedence, which was discussed in an earlier lesson in regard to calculations. In this case, precedence makes sure that the inner functions are called and return their results, which are then passed to the outer function as arguments. Precedence affects functions in the same way that parentheses affect calculations, and can be carried out to as many levels as you need.

Refactoring

The process that was just performed—separating a unit of code into a set of separate functions—is called *refactoring*. This is a critical activity when creating a complex program, especially when doing so by evolving it from a simpler form.

Many programmers believe that the act of improving (often called *enhancing*) or repairing a program inevitably makes that program more complex and harder to understand. However, if maintenance of this sort is used as an opportunity for refactoring, it can actually improve the program. And some programmers (the author included) believe that refactoring programs is a worthwhile activity in itself, separate from enhancement or repair.

In this case, the activity of refactoring is fairly simple. In fact, if you look at the example as it stood at the end of the last lesson, you can see that the whitespace in the program was a useful guide as to where to clip out code to put in a function.

Functions should have maximum *cohesion* (every statement directed toward the goal identified by the function name) and minimal *coupling* (dependence on specific actual argument values). When deciding whether a line of code should be moved into a function, these are the critical factors to consider.

> **Whitespace Indicates Cohesion**   When you are look-
> ing for a section of code to refactor, whitespace,
> whether it takes the form of braces or blank lines,
> often signals a group of closely related lines. These
> are your best candidates to move into a function.

Where You Put Function Code

C++ requires that you declare everything before you use it. Thus, a function must be declared before it is used in another function. Because of
this, the functions called by main() are typically placed in the space
above main() in C++ programs. Functions used by a function called from
main() are defined above that function, as shown here:

```
void A(void)
{
}

void C(void)
{
}

void D(void)
{
}

void B(void)
{
    C();
    D();
}

main()
{
    A();
    B();
}
```

Declaring is not always the same thing as defining. Some older C and
C++ programs use function prototypes to declare a function without
defining it.

A *prototype* is a function header with no body. It ends with a semicolon. Modern programs rarely, if ever, should use a function prototype.

You should typically start reading C++ programs at the `main()` function, and then look up above the `main()` function for the functions that are mentioned. If possible, those functions should appear in the order in which they are mentioned in the calling function. For instance, the example has

```
void Initialize(void)
float GetDividend(void)
float GetDivisor(void)
float Divide(float theDividend,float theDivisor)
int HandleNotANumberError(void)
void PauseForUserAcknowledgement(void)
```

This is essentially the order in which they are called in `main()`.

Note, however, that C++ does not require this and the compiler will not complain if you fail to follow this convention.

Global Variables

It is possible to have variables that are not in any specific function. Such a variable is called a *global variable* and can be declared at the top of the module's `.cpp` file.

Because a global variable is not "in" a particular function, it is visible to all functions. This means that any function can get or change its value.

This increases the dependence (coupling) between any functions that use the global variable, which makes maintenance more difficult. For this reason, you should avoid the use of global variables, using arguments and return values instead.

One other issue with global variables arises when local and global variables have the same name. In these instances, the local variable takes priority over the global variable, so that any changes are made to the local variable, not the global variable. In a complex program that uses many global and local variables, this can cause subtle errors that are difficult to debug. For instance, a function might accidentally change the content of (or *update*) a local variable, intending to update the global variable.

The projects in this book avoid the use of global variables, but C++ does not prevent their use and you will see them in programs written by both professionals and amateurs.

Testing

Don't forget to rerun all your tests. Regression testing is critical to making sure you haven't damaged the program by refactoring it.

Summing Up

This lesson has shown how to refactor an existing program into functions of several different types, and has demonstrated the roles of arguments and local variables. You learned that cohesion and coupling are key issues in refactoring, and that whitespace can help identify groups of lines as having the right level of cohesion to be pulled out into a separate function.

LESSON 8

Separating Code into Modules

In this lesson, you will learn how to break a single program into files that can be compiled separately.

What Is a Module?

Modules are files that can be compiled separately. The result of compiling these modules is a set of compiler output files. These files can be brought together by a *linker* to generate a single program you can run.

You've already made use of a module—iostream—in previous lessons.

Two files—a *header* file (ending in .h) and an *implementation* file (ending in .cpp)—make up a C++ module. main.cpp is the only exception to this rule. It is an implementation file that *never* has an accompanying header file.

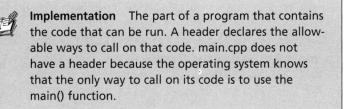

Implementation The part of a program that contains the code that can be run. A header declares the allowable ways to call on that code. main.cpp does not have a header because the operating system knows that the only way to call on its code is to use the main() function.

You have already used a header file—the iostream.h file that you include (using #include) at the top of main.cpp.

Why Use a Module?

Modules let you compile pieces of your program separately. This is important for two reasons:

1. When the program gets big, you only have to recompile the pieces you change; this saves time.

2. You can share your modules with other programmers and they can leverage the code you've created in the same way that you use the iostream library.

What Is in a Header File?

Header files tell the compiler what is in the implementation module, such as the names and arguments of functions, and definitions of constants and data types.

The functions named in the header file are *public*, because any user of the module can see them. The implementation file, however, can contain functions not mentioned in the header file that cannot be used by anything other than the module implementation. Such functions are referred to as *private*.

Making a Header File

It's time to split a few functions from the example into separate modules. Let's start with the module that will hold the PauseForUserAcknowledgement() function—PromptModule.h (see Listing 8.1).

LISTING 8.1   Header for PromptModule

```
1: #ifndef PromptModuleH
2: #define PromptModuleH
3:
4: void PauseForUserAcknowledgement(void);
5:
6: #endif
```

ANALYSIS Line 1 contains a special preprocessor instruction. It means "if not defined." When the name that follows #ifndef (that is, PromptModuleH) is not yet defined in the program, the lines from here to #endif will be passed on to the compiler.

Line 2 is what makes line 1 useful. With this, the symbol PromptModuleH is defined. If the header were included a second time in the same program, line 1 would cause the preprocessor to check its list of defined symbols, and it would see that PromptModuleH has been defined. Therefore, the code between line 1 and line 6 would not be passed to the compiler a second time.

(Note that lines 1, 2, and 6 *never* go to the compiler. They are "eaten" by the preprocessor.)

Why are lines 1, 2, and 6 so important? Imagine two library modules that use another library module such as iostream. Imagine if both of those modules were included in main.cpp. The header would be duplicated and the compiler would see two occurrences of the declaration of cout and would be unable to decide between them. Use #ifndef, #define, and #endif in every header you write.

Let's move to line 4, the core of the header file. This is a function prototype, which was discussed in the previous lesson. You can identify it as a prototype because it has no body and ends with a semicolon. It provides enough information for the compiler to ensure that a call to this function has been correctly set up with the right types for the arguments and the expected return value.

What Does an Implementation File Look Like?

Implementation files are a lot like main.cpp, except that they include their own header file as well as any others they need.

Standard C++ requires that there be something in an implementation file. There doesn't have to be anything more than a #include of its header file, but it usually contains substantial code.

Listing 8.2 is the implementation for the PromptModule.h.

LISTING 8.2   Implementation for `PromptModule`

```
 1: #include <iostream>
 2:
*3: #include "PromptModule.h"
 4:
 5: using namespace std;
 6:
 7: void PauseForUserAcknowledgement(void)
 8: {
 9:     // Note: You must type something before Enter
10:     char StopCharacter;
11:     cout << endl << "Press a key and \"Enter\": ";
12:     cin >> StopCharacter;
13: }
```

ANALYSIS Line 3 includes `iostream` and the module header file, line 5 uses the `std` namespace, and the function itself is identical to the one that was in `main.cpp`.

You use a different form for the `#include` of the `PromptModule.h` than you used for `iostream`. This is because `iostream` is a standard include file in a standard location, while `PromptModule.h` is in the current directory. The double quotes tell the preprocessor to look for a header in the current directory, and, if it is not found there, to look in any other directories provided to the compiler through its command line (see your compiler documentation for how to indicate additional directories to be searched). The `.h` extension must be specified at the end of the header filename in this form.

As you can see, you really don't need to change much to use separate compilation. But you might want to alter some names, just to be safe.

Making a Library Changes Your Names

Remember the function `Initialize()`, which was used to prepare `cin` for throwing exceptions? What if you moved error handling out to a module of its own, and some other library or main program wanted to use that common name? This could be a problem.

You have already seen a way to deal with this possibility: namespaces. That's the solution `iostream` uses and it will work perfectly for this situation.

The form of a namespace declaration is

```
namespace namespacename
{
    statements
};
```

Listing 8.3 is the new header file.

LISTING 8.3 Header for `ErrorHandlingModule`

```
 1: #ifndef ErrorHandlingModuleH
 2: #define ErrorHandlingModuleH
 3:
*4: namespace SAMSErrorHandling
*5: {
 6:     void Initialize(void);
 7:     int HandleNotANumberError(void); // Returns error code
*8: }
 9:
10: #endif
```

The implementation file appears in Listing 8.4.

LISTING 8.4 Implementation for `ErrorHandlingModule`

```
 1: #include <iostream>
*2: #include "ErrorHandlingModule.h"
 3:
*4: namespace SAMSErrorHandling
*5: {
 6:     using namespace std;
 7:
 8:     void Initialize(void)
 9:     {
10:         cin.exceptions(cin.failbit);
11:     }
12:
13:     int HandleNotANumberError(void) // Returns error code
14:     {
15:         cerr << "Input error - not a number?" << endl;
```

LISTING 8.4   Continued

```
16:
17:         cin.clear(); // Clear error state from the stream
18:
19:         // Eat the bad input so we can pause the program
20:         char BadInput[5];
21:         cin >> BadInput;
22:
23:         return 1; // An error occurred
24:     }
*25: }
```

ANALYSIS You can see how the namespace declaration in the header file (lines 4, 5, and 8 of Listing 8.3) wraps the prototypes and how the namespace declaration in the implementation file (lines 4, 5, and 25 of Listing 8.4) wraps all the functions.

Don't forget to go back and add a namespace declaration to the PromptModule header. The namespace there will be SAMSPrompt.

The name you pick for the namespace should be unique and meaningful at the same time. It should also be something that makes sense when joined to the name of the module functions, as you will see later when the calls have been modified to use the namespace as a qualifier to the function names.

Calling the Functions

The only difference that results from calling the functions in the new modules is the need to qualify function names with their namespace. Listing 8.5 shows the new main.cpp.

LISTING 8.5   main.cpp Calling on Separately Compiled Modules

```
1: #include <iostream>
2:
*3: #include "PromptModule.h"
*4: #include "ErrorHandlingModule.h"
5:
6: using namespace std;
```

LISTING 8.5   Continued

```
 7:
 8: float GetDividend(void)
 9: {
10:     float Dividend = 0;
11:
12:     cout << "Dividend: ";
13:     cin >> Dividend;
14:
15:     return Dividend;
16: }
17:
18: float GetDivisor(void)
19: {
20:     float Divisor = 1;
21:
22:     cout << "Divisor: ";
23:     cin >> Divisor;
24:
25:     return Divisor;
26: }
27:
28: float Divide
29:     (const float theDividend,const float theDivisor)
30: {
31:     return (theDividend/theDivisor);
32: }
33:
34: int main(int argc, char* argv[])
35: {
*36:     SAMSErrorHandling::Initialize();
37:
38:     float ReturnCode = 0;
39:
40:     try
41:     {
42:         float Dividend = GetDividend();
43:         float Divisor = GetDivisor();
44:
45:         cout << Divide(Dividend,Divisor) << endl;
46:     }
47:     catch (...)
48:     {
*49:         ReturnCode =
50:             SAMSErrorHandling::HandleNotANumberError();
```

LISTING 8.5   Continued

```
51:    };
52:
*53:   SAMSPrompt::PauseForUserAcknowledgement();
54:    return ReturnCode;
55: }
```

ANALYSIS   You can see in lines 36, 49, and 53 that the function names
are prefixed with the name of the namespace followed by a
double colon. This double colon is called the *scope resolution operator*,
and it tells the compiler that the name of the function is found in the specified namespace. Later, you will see the same operator used in connection
with object classes as well.

You'll notice the absence of a using statement for these new namespaces.
In general, the using statement defeats the purpose of namespaces,
because it mingles names from all namespaces together.

You'll also notice that some functions remain in main.cpp; these don't
seem likely candidates for use in other applications.

Compiling Separately

There are no standards for compiler or linker command names. The following commands compile the modules and link them together using a
fictional compiler (cppcompiler) and linker (cpplinker) under Windows:

```
cppcompiler PromptModule.cpp
cppcompiler ErrorHandlingModule.cpp
cppcompiler Main.cpp
cpplinker Calculator.exe Main.obj PromptModule.obj
➥ErrorHandlingModule.obj
```

A compiler typically produces an *intermediate* file, whose name often
ends in .obj or .o (it is sometimes called an *object* file even though it has
nothing to do with object-oriented programming). The linker combines
these files into an *executable* file (under Windows a .exe file, under Unix
a file with no extension). The operating system will be able to run this
executable file.

Now, if you change only the ErrorHandlingModule, you can compile it alone and link it with the others:

```
cppcompiler ErrorHandlingModule.cpp
cpplinker Calculator.exe Main.obj PromptModule.obj
➡ErrorHandlingModule.obj
```

The other modules may have been last compiled days earlier. In a large system with tens or hundreds of modules, this can be a time-saver.

For your compile and link commands and their options, see your compiler documentation.

Testing

Breaking a program into modules is a form of refactoring. Don't forget to run regression tests to make sure that you haven't caused a problem by splitting things up.

Summing Up

This lesson has shown how to separate an existing program into separately compilable modules, how to use #include for your own modules, how to safely use the same name in multiple modules using the namespace statement, and how to use the scope resolution operator to refer to the namespace that holds a function.

LESSON 9
do/while
Loops

In this lesson, you'll learn how to cause sections of your code to run repeatedly.

Where You Are

You have made structural adjustments to prepare the program for greater size and complexity. Now you will generalize the program to handle any number of divisions by looping.

Doing Things More Than Once

Currently, each time you want to perform a division, you have to run the program. Fortunately, C++ offers several control structures, similar to the `if` statement, that repeatedly run the code in a block (this is called a *loop*). Loops use a `bool` expression to control whether the repetition should continue. This means that the program can perform its activity many times without stopping.

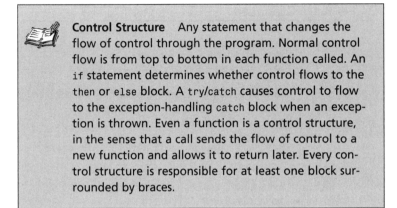

Control Structure   Any statement that changes the flow of control through the program. Normal control flow is from top to bottom in each function called. An if statement determines whether control flows to the then or else block. A try/catch causes control to flow to the exception-handling catch block when an exception is thrown. Even a function is a control structure, in the sense that a call sends the flow of control to a new function and allows it to return later. Every control structure is responsible for at least one block surrounded by braces.

Doing Things at Least Once

In many cases, you want to do something at least once and perhaps many times. This is best handled by the do/while loop.

The form of this loop is

```
do
{
    statements
}
while (condition);
```

Let's have a look at its use in the main() function of the division calculator (see Listing 9.1).

LISTING 9.1   A do/while Loop in main()

```
 1: int main(int argc, char* argv[])
 2: {
 3:     SAMSErrorHandling::Initialize();
 4:
*5:     do // At least once...
*6:     {
```

LISTING 9.1   Continued

```
 7:            try
 8:            {
 9:                float Dividend = GetDividend();
10:                float Divisor = GetDivisor();
11:
12:                cout << Divide(Dividend,Divisor) << endl;
13:            }
14:            catch (...)
15:            {
16:                SAMSErrorHandling::HandleNotANumberError();
17:            };
*18:       }
*19:       while (SAMSPrompt::UserWantsToContinue
              ➥("More division? "));
20:
21:       return 0;
22: }
```

ANALYSIS   Lines 5–6 and 18–19 make up the loop control structure.
Line 5 indicates the beginning of the loop, line 6 is the brace
that starts the block affected by the loop, line 18 is the brace that ends the
block affected by the loop, and line 19 is the expression that determines
whether repetition continues. It calls SAMSPrompt::
UserWantsToContinue(), a new function in the PromptModule.

This program's output is as follows:

OUTPUT

```
Dividend: 2
Divisor: 3
0.666667

More division?  - Press "n" and "Enter" to stop: y
Dividend: 6
Divisor: 2
3

More division?  - Press "n" and "Enter" to stop: n
```

You can see here how the prompt to continue comes after the request for
input and the display of results.

The Looping Condition

The while indicates that the loop will continue as long as the bool expression is true. This loop is controlled by the bool result returned by a function call.

The function UserWantsToContinue, added to the PromptModule SAMSPrompt namespace, is relatively simple. It gets a message as a parameter and returns a bool result. Listing 9.2 shows this function.

LISTING 9.2   UserWantsToContinue in PromptModule

```
 1:     bool UserWantsToContinue
            ➥(const char *theThingWeAreDoing)
 2:     {
 3:         char DoneCharacter;
 4:
 5:         cout <<
 6:             endl <<
 7:             theThingWeAreDoing <<
 8:             " - Press \"n\" and \"Enter\" to stop: ";
 9:
10:         cin >> DoneCharacter;
11:
12:         return (DoneCharacter != 'n'); // true when not "n"
13:     }
```

ANALYSIS   Most of this new function is familiar code, almost identical to the PauseForUserAcknowledgement() function in the same module and namespace. (The PauseForUserAcknowledgement() function call is no longer made in main.cpp because there is no need for it to ask twice whether you want to stop.)

There is a difference, however, at line 12, where the function returns the result of a bool expression. That expression has a true value if the character input by the user is not the character n. Note that the != operator means "not equal to."

The character literal 'n' is enclosed in single quotes to tell the compiler that it is a character literal rather than a string literal. (The compiler will complain if you use a string here.) That's part of C++ strong typing, and provides extra safety.

This listing contains one other item of interest: In line 1 a string is passed to the function as the formal argument theThingWeAreDoing. This will make it a better library function—now, you can use the function for any message.

If you look closely at this formal argument, you will see that it is a const char *, which means (loosely) "a string that cannot be changed."

Placement of the try/catch

The program's try/catch block is inside the loop. This means that the program will not stop, even if the user enters something that is not a number, because the exception handler will display its message and then let control flow to the line following catch, which is the while at the end of the loop.

If you moved the try/catch block outside the loop you would have the code shown in Listing 9.3.

LISTING 9.3   try/catch Outside the Loop

```
1:        try
2:        {
3:            do // At least once...
4:            {
5:                float Dividend = GetDividend();
6:                float Divisor = GetDivisor();
7:
8:                cout << Divide(Dividend,Divisor) << endl;
9:            }
10:           while (SAMSPrompt::UserWantsToContinue
                  ➡("More division? "));
11:       }
12:       catch (...)
13:       {
14:           SAMSErrorHandling::HandleNotANumberError();
15:       };
```

If you implemented this alternative and the user entered a letter instead of a number, control would leap out of the loop to line 12, the catch block code would run, control would flow to the line after the catch code (line 15), and the program would go on to stop at the end of main(). This is not useful for the program you're working on in this book, but handling a *fatal error*—where the program cannot safely continue to run—may require this.

Doing Things Zero or More Times

The do/while loop works fine as long as you can be absolutely sure that users really ran the program with the intent of doing at least one calculation. But what if they ran the program by accident and want to stop right away?

You can use the while loop in this situation. It requires only a minor change to the main() function in Listing 9.1, as shown in Listing 9.4.

LISTING 9.4 A while Loop

```
 1: int main(int argc, char* argv[])
 2: {
 3:     SAMSErrorHandling::Initialize();
 4:
*5:     while (SAMSPrompt::UserWantsToContinue("Divide? "))
*6:     {
 7:         try
 8:         {
 9:             float Dividend = GetDividend();
10:             float Divisor = GetDivisor();
11:
12:             cout << Divide(Dividend,Divisor) << endl;
13:         }
14:         catch (...)
15:         {
16:             SAMSErrorHandling::HandleNotANumberError();
17:         };
*18:     };
19:
20:     return 0;
21: }
```

ANALYSIS Here, lines 5, 6, and 18 are the ones that count. (This actually shortens the program by one line.)

You'll notice that this loop puts the while at the beginning. Now it prompts the user right away. This requires a change to the prompt string, because "More division?" doesn't make sense as the first thing to ask a user.

If the user responds with anything other than n, the program does what is in the loop. If the user responds with n, control flows to line 20 and the program stops.

The while loop, unlike the do loop, ends with a simple closing brace (line 18). There is no keyword or condition at the end, because both the keyword and the condition are at the top. Running the while loop produces the following:

OUTPUT

```
Divide?  - Press "n" and "Enter" to stop: y
Dividend: 2
Divisor: 3
0.666667

Divide?  - Press "n" and "Enter" to stop: y
Dividend: 6
Divisor: 2
3

More division?  - Press "n" and "Enter" to stop: n
```

Here, you can see that the program asks users whether they want to continue right away.

In this case the choice between a do/while loop and a while loop is simply a matter of taste. The program can stick with the do/while loop for now, but you will see that the while loop has plenty of uses.

Summing Up

This lesson has shown how to use loops and how to think about exceptions in the context of a loop. You've studied do/while loops, which run their code one or more times, and while loops, which run their code zero or more times.

LESSON 10

Nested Loops and Complex bool Expressions

In this lesson, you will learn to set up more complex decision-making capabilities in your program.

Nesting Loops

Just as if statements and other control structures such as try/catch can be nested within each other, so can loops. However, just as with if statements, this can be a bad idea, and should lead you to consider refactoring the inner loop into a function of its own.

As an example of this, you might create a variant of the UserWantsToContinue() function. This would contain a loop that would only end when the user entered either y or n. No longer could any character other than y be used to mean "continue." Listing 10.1 shows such a function.

LISTING 10.1 UserWantsToContinueYOrN in PromptModule

```
  1:    bool UserWantsToContinueYOrN
            ➥(const char *theThingWeAreDoing)
  2:    {
  3:        char DoneCharacter;
  4:
 *5:        do
 *6:        {
  7:            cout <<
  8:                endl <<
```

LISTING 10.1   Continued

```
 9:                theThingWeAreDoing <<
10:                " - Press \"n\" and \"Enter\" to stop: ";
11:
12:        cin >> DoneCharacter;
13:
*14:        if
*15:        (
*16:            !
*17:            (
*18:                (DoneCharacter == 'y')
*19:                ||
*20:                (DoneCharacter == 'n')
*21:            )
*22:        )
*23:        {
*24:            cout <<
               ➥"...Error - " <<
               ➥"please enter \"y\" or \"n\"." <<
               ➥endl;
*25:        };
*26:        }
*27:        while
*28:        (
*29:            !
*30:            (
*31:                (DoneCharacter == 'y')
*32:                ||
*33:                (DoneCharacter == 'n')
*34:            )
*35:        );
36:
37:        return (DoneCharacter != 'n');
38:    }
```

ANALYSIS   Here you see a common pattern. First, lines 7–12 prompt. Then, lines 14–22 check to see whether the input is okay— the code in these lines means "the done character is not y or n" (the ! operator means "not" and the || operator means "or"). If it isn't okay, line 24 displays an error message. Lines 27–35 check the condition again to determine whether the prompt needs to be repeated. This section of code must use exactly the same condition as the if statement.

Because there are a number of nested parentheses in these expressions, the code uses them like braces. While this takes up a lot of lines, it prevents errors in matching up parentheses and operators: If you look straight down from an open parenthesis, you see the corresponding closing parenthesis. Easy, isn't it? Compare it with the alternative

```
(!((DoneCharacter == 'y')||(DoneCharacter == 'n')))
```

and you can see why you might prefer to spend extra lines for extra clarity.

Here's one other item to note: The if statement on line 14 does not have an else. If this statement's bool expression is false, control flows right to the next statement after the true block.

Relational Operators

What exactly is the relationship between these "not" and "or" operators? Is there an "and" operator, and is it useful here? Isn't this excessively complex? Not if you approach it carefully.

First, let's recap the simple bool expression in a little more detail. Remember that a bool expression can be true or false. There are six bool *relational operators,* used to compare values. Like +, they are infix operators, so they have an operand to the left and an operand to the right. Table 10.1 shows their names, symbols, examples of their use, and the example values.

TABLE 10.1   The Relational Operators

Name	Operator	Sample	Value
Equal to	==	100 == 50;	false
		50 == 50;	true
Not equal to	!=	100 != 50;	true
		50 != 50;	false
Greater than	>	100 > 50;	true
		50 > 50;	false

TABLE 10.1   Continued

Name	Operator	Sample	Value
Greater than	`>=`	`100 >= 50;`	`true`
or equal to		`50 >= 50;`	`true`
Less than	`<`	`100 < 50;`	`false`
		`50 < 50;`	`false`
Less than	`<=`	`100 <= 50;`	`false`
or equal to		`50 <= 50;`	`true`

There are also two infix operators used to create complex `bool` expressions—`&&` (and) and `||` (or).

`&&` means that when its two operands are `true`, the expression is `true`; if one or both operands are `false`, the expression is `false`. So `(true && true) == true`, `(true && false) == false`, and `(false && false) == false`.

`||` means that when either operand is `true`, the expression is `true`. So `(true || true) == true`, `(true || false) == true`, and `(false || false) == false`.

And don't forget the prefix unary `bool` operator—the bang operator (`!`), which means "not." If an expression is `true`, `!` makes it `false`; if an expression is `false`, `!` makes it `true`. This is called *negation.*

Now take a closer look at the complex `bool` expressions, shown in Listing 10.2. Remember, you want to print an error and loop when a user enters anything that is not a *y* or an *n*. (Note that when parentheses are used, you have to read an expression from the inside out.)

LISTING 10.2   The Condition in Detail

```
*15:             (
*16:                 !
*17:                 (
*18:                     (DoneCharacter == 'y')
*19:                     ||
```

LISTING 10.2   Continued

```
*20:                       (DoneCharacter == 'n')
*21:                   )
*22:               )
```

ANALYSIS Lines 18 and 20 are the innermost expressions. When a correct character is entered, one of the expressions will be `true`. When an incorrect character is entered, neither of them will be `true`.

Line 19 is the "or" that combines the two expressions into one. If either of the expressions is `true` (the user enters a valid character), the result of the "or" expression will be `true`; if an invalid character is entered, it will be `false`.

Line 16 negates the result using the bang operator. The reason for this can be confusing, so read carefully.

Remember that the `if` statement and the loop will only perform their blocks when the condition is `true`. You want this condition to be `true` when the input is *invalid*, but the expression is `true` when the input character is *valid*. Thus, you must negate the `true` result using the bang operator. This makes the condition `false` when valid characters have been input and `true` when they have not.

If you read the expression as if it were natural language, it is a little easier to see how this works:

If not (DoneCharacter is y *or DoneCharacter is* n*) then you have an error.*

Here's an alternative form:

If (DoneCharacter is not y *and DoneCharacter is not* n*) then you have an error.*

Written in code, this would be

```
(DoneCharacter != 'y') && (DoneCharacter != 'n')
```

This has the same effect as the first form. Some people find the "and" in this style of expression a little harder to understand. Settle on one style or the other and stick with it consistently.

Simplifying by Using a **bool** Variable

The big danger in the earlier example is that, because you've put the same **bool** expression in two places, you will cause an accident if you do not make or keep the two expressions identical. This could lead to a serious and hard-to-solve problem in your program during repair or enhancement. You can use a **bool** variable to avoid it, as shown in Listing 10.3.

LISTING 10.3   UserWantsToContinueYOrN in PromptModule with a **bool** Expression

```
 1:     bool UserWantsToContinueYOrN
           ➥(const char *theThingWeAreDoing)
 2:     {
 3:         char DoneCharacter;
*4:         bool InvalidCharacterWasEntered = false;
 5:
 6:         do
 7:         {
 8:            cout <<
 9:                endl <<
10:                theThingWeAreDoing <<
11:                " - Press \"n\" and \"Enter\" to stop: ";
12:
13:            cin >> DoneCharacter;
14:
*15:           InvalidCharacterWasEntered =
*16:               !
*17:               (
*18:                   (DoneCharacter == 'y')
*19:                   ||
*20:                   (DoneCharacter == 'n')
*21:               );
22:
*23:           if (InvalidCharacterWasEntered)
24:           {
25:               cout <<
                   ➥"...Error - " <<
                   ➥"please enter \"y\" or \"n\"." <<
                   ➥endl;
```

LISTING 10.3   Continued

```
26:              };
27:      }
*28:     while (InvalidCharacterWasEntered);
29:
30:      return (DoneCharacter != 'n');
31:  }
```

ANALYSIS Let's start with line 4, which defines a bool variable for the purpose of saving the result of the bool expression. Your first reaction might be to wonder why this variable, which is to be used as the loop condition, is defined outside the loop.

An important rule of C++ is that a variable declared inside a block (remember, a block is a set of lines surrounded by braces) is created when the control flow reaches the opening brace, and disappears when control flows past the closing brace. If you put your bool variable inside the loop, while cannot use it in the condition, and the result is a compiler message that looks like this:

```
[C++ Error] PromptModule.cpp(34):
➥E2451 Undefined symbol 'InvalidCharacterWasEntered'
```

Next, the bool expression has been moved out of the if condition and onto lines 15–21, which assign the result to the variable.

In line 23, the if statement tests the variable to see whether there is a problem and therefore a need to produce the error message.

Line 28 uses the same variable to decide whether the loop needs to repeat, prompting the user again.

This is much safer than using two identical expressions, of course. And you've given a name to the expression, so it's much easier to understand what it is intended to represent.

Don't forget to add the prototype to the header and modify main.cpp to use this new and improved function. And, of course, don't forget regression testing.

Summing Up

This lesson has shown how to use more complex bool expressions. You learned how to use a function to control the complexity of nesting loops inside other loops. You also learned how to use bool variables to avoid duplicating a bool expression in two or more control statements (such as an if statement and a do/while loop), thus making your programs easier to understand and maintain.

LESSON 11

switch Statements, static Variables, and runtime_errors

In this lesson, you will learn about the switch *statement. You will also discover the use of* static *local variables and how to throw the* runtime_error *exception.*

switch Statements

if and else...if combinations can become quite confusing when nested deeply, and C++ offers an alternative. Unlike if, which evaluates one value, switch statements enable you to change control flow based on any of a number of different values for an expression. The general form of the switch statement is

```
switch (expression)
{
    case constantexpression1: statement; break;
    case constantexpression2: statement; break;
    ....
    case constantexpression3: statement; break;
    default: statement;
}
```

expression is any legal C++ expression resulting in a character or other simple result (such as int or float), and the *statement*s are any legal C++ statements or blocks.

switch evaluates *expression* and compares the result to each of the case *constantexpressions*. These can be, and usually are, literals, but they can be something as complex as 3+x*y, as long as x and y are const variables.

If one of the case values matches the expression, control flows to that case's statement and continues from there to the end of the switch block until a break statement is encountered. If nothing matches, control flows to the optional default statement. If there is no default and no matching value, the statement has no effect and control flows on.

> **The default Case in switch Statements** It is almost always a good idea to have a default case in switch statements. If you have no other need for the default, use it to test for the supposedly impossible case and throw an exception.

It is important to note that if there is no break at the end of a case's statement or block, control will flow through to the next case. The absence of a break is sometimes intentional and necessary, but usually indicates a common error with surprising effects. If you decide to let control flow through, be sure to put a comment indicating that you didn't just forget the break.

Generalizing the Calculator

You have been writing a lot of code to support performing division. Now you are ready to take a major step and make this simple program into a full-blown calculator. And the switch statement will be an important part of that change.

Let's start with the main() function, shown in Listing 11.1.

LISTING 11.1   main() as a Real Calculator

```
1: int main(int argc, char* argv[])
2: {
3:     SAMSErrorHandling::Initialize();
4:
```

LISTING 11.1   Continued

```
 5:     do
 6:     {
 7:         try
 8:         {
*9:             char Operator = GetOperator();
*10:            float Operand = GetOperand();
11:
*12:            cout << Accumulate(Operator,Operand) << endl;
13:         }
*14:        catch (runtime_error RuntimeError)
*15:        {
*16:            SAMSErrorHandling::HandleRuntimeError
                    ➥(RuntimeError);
*17:        }
18:        catch (...)
19:        {
20:            SAMSErrorHandling::HandleNotANumberError();
21:        };
22:     }
23:     while (SAMSPrompt::UserWantsToContinueYorN("More? "));
24:
25:     return 0;
26: }
```

ANALYSIS   The changes start in lines 9 and 10, which aren't getting divisors and dividends anymore. This is now going to be a real calculator, so those lines get an "operator" and an "operand." The names of the functions and variables have been changed accordingly. Also note that the Operator is a single char.

Line 12 applies the Operator and Operand to an accumulator through the Accumulate() function. This function "accumulates" the current state of the calculation and returns the result after each new operator and operand is processed so that the result can be displayed by line 12. This is the same way your desktop or pocket calculator works.

Lines 14–17 catch a new type of exception—the runtime_error from the Standard C++ library—by declaring a variable of the appropriate type in the catch(). The catch for this exception goes before the old catch, because when you want to catch a specific type of exception, you must do so before catch (...). This is required because the ellipsis (...) means that the following section handles any leftover exceptions.

The runtime_error exception signals that the user entered something that should have been an operator, but was not recognized as one (for instance, a question mark would cause this exception).

OUTPUT

```
Operator: +
Operand: 3
3

More?  - Press "n" and "Enter" to stop: y
Operator: a
Operand: 3
Error - Invalid operator - must be one of +,-,* or /

More?  - Press "n" and "Enter" to stop: y
Operator: +
Operand: a
Input error - input may not have been a number.

More?  - Press "n" and "Enter" to stop: y
Operator: -
Operand: 2
1

More?  - Press "n" and "Enter" to stop: n
```

The switch Statement

There's nothing in GetOperator() and GetOperand() that you haven't seen before in GetDivisor() and GetDividend() (except that GetOperator() obtains and returns a char), so let's skip those functions and go right to Accumulate() and its switch statement, shown in Listing 11.2.

LISTING 11.2   Accumulate() in main.cpp

```
1: float Accumulate
        ➡(const char theOperator,const float theOperand)
2: {
3:     static float myAccumulator = 0;
            ➡// Initialized to 0 when the program starts
```

LISTING 11.2 Continued

```
4:
5:      switch (theOperator)
6:      {
7:          case '+':
                myAccumulator = myAccumulator + theOperand;
                break;

8:          case '-':
                myAccumulator = myAccumulator - theOperand;
                break;

9:          case '*':
                myAccumulator = myAccumulator * theOperand;
                break;

10:         case '/':
                myAccumulator = myAccumulator / theOperand;
                break;
11:
12:         default:
13:             throw
14:                 runtime_error
15:                     ("Error - Invalid operator");
16:     };
17:
18:     return myAccumulator;
19: }
```

ANALYSIS Here you can see the switch statement in lines 5–16, which look for each of the standard operator symbols and perform the corresponding operation on the accumulator for each.

One of the interesting things about the accumulator is that on each call, the value of myAccumulator is based not only on the current function's actual arguments, but also on previous calls to Accumulate().

How can this be?

static Local Variables

Line 3 declares the accumulator to be a static float. static means that unlike a normal local variable, which is created when the function is called and disappears when control flows back to the caller, this variable is created and initialized when the program starts and does not disappear until the program stops. In fact, it is just like a global variable, except that it is hidden away inside the function, which means it is not susceptible to the pitfalls of using global variables.

Each time you add, subtract, multiply, or divide against this variable, the value you act on is the one you finished with the last time you called the function. You will later see that this idea is very similar to a key concept in object-oriented programming called *encapsulation* or *information hiding*, which is why it is introduced here.

Because the function owns this variable, but it is not really a local variable, use the special prefix "my" for the variable name as a reminder. As with using "the" to prefix formal arguments, this convention keeps you from having to hunt around the program for the source of the value.

Throwing an Exception Yourself

Line 13 has a special feature as well. It creates and throws an exception when the operator does not match anything in the switch statement. Use the throw statement with the Standard C++ library runtime_error exception object for this purpose, and provide a message as part of the exception. Remember that line 14 of main() catches this specific type of exception.

Dealing with the New Exception

Handling this new exception requires a new function in the ErrorHandlingModule's SAMSErrorHandling namespace.

This function, shown in Listing 11.3, is pretty simple.

LISTING 11.3   HandleRuntimeError() in
ErrorHandlingModule

```
1:    int HandleRuntimeError(runtime_error theRuntimeError)
2:    {
3:       cerr <<
4:          theRuntimeError.what() <<
5:          endl;
```

LISTING **11.3**   Continued

```
6:
7:        return 1;
8:    }
```

ANALYSIS   Line 1 is the function header and shows the formal argument theRuntimeError, which is of type runtime_error. Line 4 uses the standard exception what() function to get the error message you put into the exception object in lines 14 and 15 of Accumulate(). Line 7 follows the pattern of the other error-handling functions and returns an int 1, which you can use to set a return code in main() if you desire.

Naturally, the prototype for this function has to be added to the header for the module—don't forget to do that!

To use runtime_error, you need to change ErrorHandlingModule to #include <exception>. You must also add using namespace std wherever the exception is mentioned. You must do these things in both the header file and implementation file of ErrorHandlingModule.

Summing Up

You now have a complete calculator. It lets you enter an operator and a number and it accumulates the effects of these inputs in a static local variable of a function. It uses the switch statement to determine what to do to the accumulator, based on an operator character entered by the user. When it gets an invalid operator, it throws a Standard C++ library exception (runtime_error) that it handles with a new and separate catch of runtime_error in main(). It reports the exception with a new function in the ErrorHandlingModule.

Arrays, Loops, and the Increment and Decrement Operators

In this lesson, you will learn how to create and use arrays and how the for *loop can be used to access the elements of an array.*

Using an Array to Create a Calculator Tape

The calculator program will make use of an array to keep track of what has been entered so far. You'll use it to create a "calculator tape," with an entry for each operator/operand pair entered.

An *array* is a named sequence of locations for data. Each location is called an *element* and each element holds the same type of data. You use an element by specifying the name of the array and an *index* that is the numeric offset of the element in the array; this starts at zero.

You define an array by identifying the type of data it will hold in each element, followed by the array name and the count of elements it will contain, in brackets—for instance, int SomeArray[3]. The count can be any literal, constant, or constant expression.

You reference an element to get or change its value using the array name and the element sequence (0 is the first element) in brackets—for instance, int x = SomeArray[0];. An element reference can be on the left- or right-hand side of an assignment statement, just like a variable.

The Tape

The Tape() function is fairly simple, and is coded in main.cpp.

LISTING 12.1   Tape() in main.cpp

```
 1: void Tape(const char theOperator,const float theOperand)
 2: {
 3:     static const int myTapeSize = 20; // Array size
 4:
 5:     static char myOperator[myTapeSize]; // Operator part
 6:     static float myOperand[myTapeSize]; // Operand part
 7:
 8:     static int myNumberOfEntries = 0; // What's in tape now
 9:
10:     // Remember that arrays start with element 0
11:     // And that the highest element is the size - 1;
12:
13:     if (theOperator != '?') // Add to the tape
14:     {
15:         if (myNumberOfEntries  < myTapeSize) // We have room
16:         {
17:             myOperator[myNumberOfEntries] = theOperator;
18:             myOperand[myNumberOfEntries] = theOperand;
19:             myNumberOfEntries++;
20:         }
21:         else // About to overflow the array
22:         {
23:             throw runtime_error[ccc]
                    ("Error - Out of room on the tape.");
24:         };
25:     }
26:     else // Display the tape
27:     {
28:         for
              ➥(
                  ➥int Index = 0;
                  ➥Index < myNumberOfEntries;
                  ➥Index++
              ➥)
29:         {
30:             cout <<
                  ➥myOperator[Index] << "," <<
                  ➥myOperand[Index] <<
                  ➥endl;
```

LISTING 12.1   Continued

```
31:          };
32:     };
33: }
```

ANALYSIS Lines 3–9 set up the tape. Notice how these are all `static` local variables, like `myAccumulator` in `Accumulate()`. Thus, they are initialized when the program starts and retain their contents from one call to the next.

Line 3 controls the maximum size of the arrays. Arrays require a constant expression to identify their size when they are created, and line 3 sets up that constant and gives it a name. Because the arrays are static, their size constant needs to be static too, or it will not have been initialized when the arrays are created at the start of the program run.

Lines 5 and 6 are the operator and operand arrays that are the actual tape. You might say they are *parallel*, because the operator in the first element of the `myOperator` array is the one used with the operand in the same element of the `myOperand` array.

Line 8 keeps a count of how many elements there are in the arrays so far. You need this because the arrays have a fixed size, and you have to throw an exception when the user has entered so many operator/operand pairs that the array will overflow. Line 32 updates this count.

Lines 10 and 11 provide a little reminder.

Line 13 checks to see whether `theOperator` is the array that causes the tape contents to be displayed. If so, control flows to line 27.

Line 15 checks to see whether there is room left on the tape. If `myNumberOfEntries == myTapeSize`, the index is about to go one past the end of the array. Rather than allow this, line 23 throws a `runtime_error` exception, which is caught in `main()`.

Line 17 starts to actually add to the tape. This line sets the appropriate element of each of the arrays using an index that is, by definition, one above the last element used—`myNumberOfEntries`. This is a C++ trick based on the fact that arrays are indexed from 0, and the element count is based on 1, so the index of the new entry is always the same as the count.

Line 19 introduces a new arithmetic operator—the double plus (++). This is the *postfix increment operator*, a very commonly used operator. It will add 1 to the variable named before it. This line updates myNumberOfEntries to the appropriate count, so you can check it the next time through and make sure that you don't overrun the array bounds.

Line 28 is in the block that is performed when theOperator is ?, which means "display the tape." In that block, a for loop is used to move through the array so that the elements can be displayed with cout.

The for Loop

The for loop combines three parts—*initialization, condition,* and *step*—into one statement at the top of the block it controls. A for statement has the following form:

```
for (initialization; condition; step)
{
    statements;
};
```

The first part of the for statement is the *initialization*. Any legal C++ statements can be put here (separated by commas), but typically this is used to create and initialize an index variable. Such a variable is most commonly an int. This part ends with a semicolon and is only performed once before the loop starts.

Next is the *condition*, which can be any legal C++ bool expression. This serves the same role as the condition in the while loop and should be read as "while Index is less than myNumberOfEntries" in the example. This part also ends with a semicolon, but it is performed at the start of every repetition.

Finally there is the *step*. Typically, the index variable is incremented or decremented here, although any legal C++ statements, separated by commas, are valid. This part is performed at the end of every repetition.

Note that the index of the loop, or any other variable declared in the initialization part of the for statement, can be used inside the loop, but not outside it. In the case of the loop at line 28 in Tape(), the variable Index cannot be used at line 32, but can be used at line 30.

Writing Past the End of an Array

When you reference an element in an array, the compiler (unfortunately) does not care whether the element actually exists. It computes how far past the first element it should go and then generates instructions that get or change that location's content. If the element is past the bounds of the array, this can be virtually anything and the results will be unpredictable. If you're lucky, your program will crash immediately or throw a bounds violation exception. If you're unlucky, you may get strange results much further on in your program run. You need to make sure that the condition in your `for` statement will cause the loop to stop before it goes past the bounds of the array. The condition expression *Index* < *NumberOfElements* is always certain to accomplish this, because the highest valid index is always one less than the count of elements in the array.

Incrementing and Decrementing

Let's look in a little more detail at line 19 of `Tape()`.

The most common value to add (or subtract) and then reassign into a variable is 1. In C++, increasing a value by 1 is called *incrementing*, and decreasing by 1 is called *decrementing*.

The increment operator (++) increases the value of its variable by 1, and the decrement operator (--) decreases it by 1. Thus, if you had a variable, x, and you wanted to increment it, you would use this statement:

```
x++;   // Start with x and increment it.
```

Both the increment operator and the decrement operator come in two styles: *prefix* and *postfix*.

Prefix   The operator is written before the variable name (++x).

Postfix   The operator is written after the variable name (x++).

In a simple statement, it doesn't matter which of these you use, but in a complex statement, when you are incrementing (or decrementing) a variable and then assigning the result to another variable, it does.

Prefix means "increment the value and then get it." Postfix means "get the value and then increment the source."

In other words, if x is an `int` whose value is 5 and you write

```
int a = ++x;
```

the program will increment x (making it 6) and then assign it to a. Thus, a is now 6 and x is now 6.

If, after doing this, you write

```
int b = x++;
```

the program will get the value in x (6) and assign it to b, and then increment x. Thus, b is now 6 but x is now 7.

This can be tricky, and you should be careful. Although the compiler will not prevent you from mixing prefix and postfix operators in confusing ways, the person who has to maintain your program might not appreciate how clever you've been.

The Calculator Tape in the Accumulator

Returning to the broader picture, Listing 12.2 shows the `Accumulate()` function in `main.cpp` with some minor changes that enable it to use the tape.

LISTING 12.2   Using the Tape in `Accumulate()`

```
1: float Accumulate
2:     (const char theOperator,const float theOperand)
3: {
4:     static float myAccumulator = 0;
            ➥// Set at program start
5:
6:     switch (theOperator)
7:     {
```

LISTING 12.2   Continued

```
 8:        case '+':
 9:            myAccumulator = myAccumulator + theOperand;
10:            break;
11:
12:        case '-':
13:            myAccumulator = myAccumulator - theOperand;
14:            break;
15:
16:        case '*':
17:            myAccumulator = myAccumulator * theOperand;
18:            break;
19:
20:        case '/':
21:            myAccumulator = myAccumulator / theOperand;
22:            break;
23:
*24:        case '?':
*25:            break;
26:
27:        default:
28:            throw
29:                runtime_error
30:                    ("Error - Invalid operator");
31:    };
32:
*33:    Tape(theOperator,theOperand);
34:
35:    return myAccumulator;
36: }
```

ANALYSIS Line 33 records the operator and operand on the tape. Lines 24 and 25 enable the user to enter ? as an operator and cause the tape to display itself.

Summing Up

You have seen that arrays can be very useful for setting up variables that create an orderly data storage system indexed by the sequence of that data in the array. You have used two arrays to create a fixed size calculator tape. You have also looked at the increment and decrement operators and at the for loop, all of which are closely related because of the way they are used with arrays.

Lesson 13

Storage: Heaps, Stacks, and Pointing

In this lesson, you will learn how storage is allocated, the difference between heap and stack allocation, and how to use pointers effectively.

Heaps Versus Stacks

You might recall from the discussion of local variables and loops that the opening brace of a block is where variables defined inside the block are created and that the block's closing brace causes that storage to disappear. This is true for functions, loops, and if statements.

The storage for these variables is said to be "allocated on the stack."

A stack is a common "array-like" data structure whose elements are added to one end (pushed) and then taken away from that same end (popped). The compiler generates code to expand and contract a program's single stack of storage each time you call or return from a function and each time you open or close a block.

Figure 13.1 shows what happens when you call the function UserWantsToContinueYorN(), which has a parameter, a return value, and two local variables:

```
bool UserWantsToContinueYorN(const char *theThingWeAreDoing)
{
    char DoneCharacter;
    bool InvalidCharacterWasEntered = false;
```

Before the function call is made, space is pushed for the return value of the function and for the function argument.

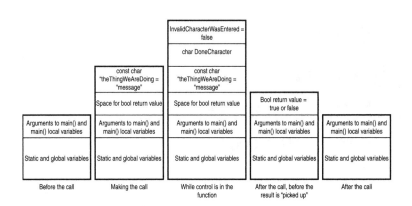

Figure 13.1 When a program calls a function, space for a return value, actual arguments, and local variables is pushed onto the stack.

When control flows to the function, local variable definitions are encountered, and space for those variables is pushed on the stack to be used as control flows through the function.

Then the function comes to an end. The return statement puts the return value in the space reserved for it. Local variables are popped off the stack. Control flows back to main(). The function call in main() gets the return value, which it puts in some local or global variable or throws away. The space for the return value is popped from the stack, and then everything is as it was.

This is a typical "stack allocation"—it is tidy and convenient, because the compiler creates all the code needed to clean up stacked variables behind the scenes, saving us the trouble.

For many programs, stack allocation is all you need. However, when you have an array that needs to vary in size, stack allocation can't do the job. The only way to "resize" an array is by creating a new array of the desired size, copying the content of the old array to the new array, getting rid of the old array space, and using the new array in its place.

Storage for this cannot come from the stack, because stack allocation does not allow you to create anything without entering a block or get rid of anything without exiting a block.

The answer to this problem is the "heap," which is represented in Figure 13.2.

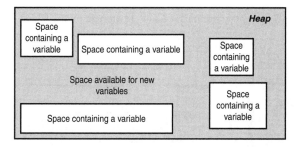

FIGURE 13.2   The heap is an area from which space can be allocated for new variables.

It is called a heap because it is a disorderly pile of available storage, only some of which may be in use at any given time.

But how do you tell the compiler that you want storage from the heap rather than from the stack? Use the special operator new:

```
type *name = new type;
```

For example:

```
char *Something = new char;
```

This reserves a space of one character in the heap, returning the location of that space.

Pointers, References, and Arrays

Astute readers will recall seeing something like the preceding definitions earlier in the book—for instance, in the arguments to main():

```
char* argv[]
```

Or the argument to UserWantsToContinueYorN():

```
char *theThingWeAreDoing
```

But what is the meaning of * in these definitions? In a definition, * should be read as "pointer to," so we can read these two lines as "pointer to an array of characters" and "pointer to a character," respectively.

Figure 13.3 shows how pointers "point" to storage on the heap.

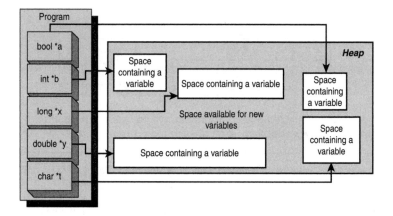

FIGURE 13.3 Pointers have a location in the heap as their value.

* is also a prefix operator that can be used outside a definition, but only with pointers. For instance:

```
char *Something = new char;
*Something = 'x';
```

In this case, * should be read as "the storage pointed to by," so we have "the storage pointed to by the pointer Something gets the value 'x' stored in it." * can also be used on the right-hand side of the assignment, as in

```
char Other = *Something;
```

This reads, "declare a local stack variable Other and set its value to the same as what is in the storage pointed to by Something." Use of * in this context is called *dereferencing*.

While it is possible to create space for simple variables in the heap, as you saw earlier, it is not something you normally need to do. Pointers really start to come into their own when they are used to represent arrays.

Arrays Are Really Pointers

The array notation is really a disguise for the use of pointers. It is perfectly valid in C++ to code

```
char SomeString[5] = "0123";
```

and then to refer to SomeString[0] (sometimes called the "zeroth character" or the "zeroth element") with a statement such as

```
char FirstCharacter = *SomeString;
```

This assigns the content of the zeroth character of SomeString to the character variable FirstCharacter, but should be avoided.

Interestingly, you can allocate an array on the heap into a pointer, and still use array notation to access its elements. This means that you can create and destroy an array using the heap. And, ultimately, this means that you can change the size of an array while the program runs.

The Tape() Arrays from the Heap

Listing 13.1 shows heap allocation for arrays within the Tape() function. This function has now been written to use the heap as the source for the myOperator and myOperand arrays.

Note   The character string 0123 is actually five characters long: 0123 followed by an implied and hidden character to signal the end of the string (the *string terminator*).

The string terminator is important because many functions in C++ libraries (and iostream) need it to tell where the string text ends.

The string terminator has a numeric value of 0. This is not the same as having the character value '0'.

Each Character Has a Numeric Value   The ASCII character set defines a numeric value for every character, with those numeric values ranging from 0 to 255. The character '0' has a numeric value of 48, while the char '\0' has a numeric value of 0.

The \ in '\0' indicates that the next value is a special value—either a numeric value such as 0, to be used to create the corresponding character, or another value such as a single or double quote, which would otherwise be impossible to put inside the quotes of a character or string literal.

Note   it is possible to shorten a string by assigning the '\0' to an array position, such as SomeString[3] = '\0';.

LISTING 13.1   Tape() Using the Heap

```
 1: void Tape(const char theOperator,const int theOperand)
 2: {
*3:     static const int myTapeChunk = 3;
 4:
*5:     static char *myOperator = new char[myTapeChunk];
*6:     static int *myOperand = new int[myTapeChunk];
 7:
*8:     static int myTapeSize = myTapeChunk;
```

LISTING 13.1   Continued

```
 9:     static int myNumberOfEntries = 0;
10:
11:     // Remember that arrays start with element 0
12:     // And that the highest element is the size - 1;
13:
*14:    switch (theOperator)
*15:    {
*16:       case '?': // Display the tape
17:
18:           for
19:              (
20:                 int Index = 0;
21:                 Index < myNumberOfEntries;
22:                 Index++
23:              )
24:           {
25:              cout <<
26:                 myOperator[Index] << "," <<
27:                 myOperand[Index] <<
28:                 endl;
29:           };
30:
31:           break;
32:
*33:       case '.': // The program is stopping, delete arrays
*34:
*35:           delete [] myOperator;
*36:           delete [] myOperand;
*37:
*38:           break;
39:
*40:       default:  // Add to the tape and expand if needed
*41:
*42:           if (myNumberOfEntries == myTapeSize) // Expand
*43:           {
*44:              // Create a destination for the expansion
*45:
*46:              char *ExpandedOperator =
*47:                 new char[myNumberOfEntries + myTapeChunk];
*48:
*49:              int *ExpandedOperand =
*50:                 new int[myNumberOfEntries + myTapeChunk];
*51:
*52:              // We use pointers to do the array copy,
*53:              // starting at the array start position.
*54:
```

LISTING 13.1   Continued

```
*55:                char *FromOperator = myOperator;
*56:                int *FromOperand = myOperand;
*57:
*58:                char *ToOperator = ExpandedOperator;
*59:                int *ToOperand = ExpandedOperand;
*60:
*61:                // Copy the old arrays to the new
*62:                // This is supposed to be faster
*63:                // than copying arrays using indexes
*64:                // but it is dangerous
*65:
*66:                for
*67:                    (
*68:                        int Index = 0;
*69:                        Index < myNumberOfEntries;
*70:                        Index++
*71:                    )
*72:                {
*73:                    *ToOperator++ = *FromOperator++;
*74:                    *ToOperand++ = *FromOperand++;
*75:                };
*76:
*77:                // Delete the old arrays
*78:
*79:                delete [] myOperator;
*80:                delete [] myOperand;
*81:
*82:                // Replace the old pointers with the new
*83:
*84:                myOperator = ExpandedOperator;
*85:                myOperand = ExpandedOperand;
*86:
*87:                // Record how big the array is now
*88:
*89:                myTapeSize+= myTapeChunk;
*90:
*91:                // Now it's safe to add a new entry
*92:            };
 93:
 94:            myOperator[myNumberOfEntries] = theOperator;
 95:            myOperand[myNumberOfEntries] = theOperand;
 96:            myNumberOfEntries++;
 97:    };
 98: }
```

ANALYSIS Keep in mind what this code is intended to do. Most of the time, it will act just like the old `Tape()`. The only time it will be different is when you run out of room in the tape. When that happens, it will create new and larger arrays for `myOperator` and `myOperand`, copy the contents of the old arrays to the new arrays, get rid of the old arrays, and replace their pointers with pointers to the new arrays. Then it will proceed as if nothing had happened.

The changes start with lines 3, 5, 6, and 8, which control how frequently the arrays will be resized (`TapeChunk` is the size of one "chunk" of array), and then creates the arrays at their initial size using `new` and the number of elements to be created (`TapeChunk` again). Line 8 remembers how big the array is now.

The new code uses a `switch` rather than an `if` control structure (line 14), because there are now three alternatives—display the tape (line 16), delete the tape because you are stopping the program (line 33), or add to the tape (line 40), possibly expanding it if it is found to have run out of room on line 43. A set of nested `if`s would be more awkward to read.

Focus on the logic for expanding the tape (line 43). First, it creates replacement arrays with `new`, supplying the new number of elements for these heap-allocated arrays in the brackets.

Lines 55–59 probably look a little odd. These lines set up pointers that will be used for the copy. The pointers are set to point to the same storage that the old and new arrays point to. Use of these extra pointers avoids disrupting the source and destination arrays during the copy performed in lines 66–75.

Lines 66–75 are a `for` loop whose purpose it is to copy all the elements from the old to the new arrays.

It could also have been written as shown in Listing 13.2.

LISTING 13.2   An Alternate Array Copy in `Tape()`

```
*66:            for
*67:              (
*68:                  int Index = 0;
*69:                  Index < myNumberOfEntries;
```

LISTING 13.2   Continued

```
*70:                    Index++
*71:                )
*72:            {
*73:                ToOperator[Index] = FromOperator[Index];
*74:                ToOperand[Index] = FromOperand[Index];
*75:            };
```

If this alternative were used, lines 66–75 would be unnecessary. So why not do it this simpler way?

An expression such as ExpandedOperator[Index] really means (*(ExpandedOperator+(Index*sizeof(char))))—that is, "the contents of the location at the position (Index times the size of a char) distant from the start of the array." For large arrays, such a large number of multiplications can drastically slow the copy. Thus, many C++ programmers use the "pointer" style of copying.

Here is one of the copy statements in this style:

```
*ToOperator++ = *FromOperator++
```

Remembering that * (also called the *dereferencing operator*) has the highest precedence and that the postfix increment operator doesn't increment until after the value has been copied, this reads, "Copy the content of the element pointed to by FromOperator to the location of the element pointed to by ToOperator. Then move each pointer to the next element."

Lines 79 and 80 get rid of the old arrays. The delete keyword is the opposite of new. The brackets tell delete that what is being deleted is an array, not just a single element of the array.

Lines 84 and 85 redirect the pointers for myOperator and myOperand to the resized array locations.

Line 96 increases the size of the variable keeping track of the maximum size of the tape by the number of elements added. It uses the special += operator, which adds the right-hand side to the left-hand side as if you had written myTapeSize = myTapeSize + myTapeChunk. (There are corresponding = operators for the other arithmetic operations: -=, *=, and /=).

Lines 94 and 95 actually add the new values to the arrays.

References

C++ offers an alternative to pointers called *references*. A reference seems like a pointer but doesn't need the * to get to the content pointed to by the pointer. It is declared with & instead of *. But it is not a pointer—it is an alternate name for a variable or a location.

Here is the definition and use of a reference:

```
1:  char &SomeReference = *(new char);
2:  SomeReference = 'x';
3:  delete &SomeReference;
4:  &SomeReference = *(new char); // This is not allowed
```

Line 1 allocates a character and sets the reference to refer to it. The compiler requires you to dereference the pointer in this initialization.

Line 2 deletes the heap storage. It uses the prefix operator & (which reads, "location of" or "address of"). The compiler requires you to do this because the reference is not a pointer to the storage—it is a name (an alias) for the storage.

The compiler produces an error on the last line. A reference must be initialized where it is defined. After that, it cannot be "reseated" to refer to anything else—which is why we don't use references for our `Tape()` array resize. But references *are* excellent for formal arguments.

Pointers Are Dangerous

Remember that the compiler doesn't care if you try to get or put the value of an element that is outside an array's size. This is because arrays are really convenient shorthand for pointers.

Pointers are just as dangerous as arrays for the same reasons. Have a look at this:

```
char *SomePointer;
*SomePointer = 'x'; // Oops.
```

What do you think this does? If you answer, "I don't know," you're right. The behavior of a program with an uninitialized pointer is undefined and unpredictable.

```
char *SomePointer = NULL;
*SomePointer = 'x'; // Oops.
```

In this case, NULL means "points to nothing." If you are lucky, the program stops. If you are unlucky, your entire system may freeze or crash. Still, NULL is often used to indicate that a pointer does not point to a real heap location. It's better than pointing to a random spot in the heap.

Deleting from the Heap

Deleting a heap-allocated pointer releases the storage it points to. delete comes in two forms: with [] (to delete an array), and without (to delete a regular variable).

Deleting is dangerous. Imagine what happens when you run this:

```
char *SomePointer = NULL;
delete SomePointer;
```

or this:

```
char *SomePointer;
delete SomePointer;
```

or:

```
char *SomePointer = new char;
delete SomePointer;
delete SomePointer;
```

or:

```
char *SomePointer = new char;
delete SomePointer;
char Stuff = *SomePointer;
```

As with using an invalid pointer or accessing beyond the end of an array, the consequences are unpredictable.

Deleting Arrays

It's a common mistake to forget to delete an array:

```
char *SomePointer = new char[25];
delete SomePointer;
```

This will delete the zeroth element of SomePointer and leave the other 24 characters of the array taking up space in the heap. Eventually, there will be no more room in the heap, and the program will stop running. This is called a *memory leak*.

Summing Up

You have just gone through one of the most difficult lessons in this book. Pointers are critical to mastering C++, but they are the cause of a large number of programming problems. You have seen how stack allocation and heap allocation differ from each other, how to get storage from the heap, how to use it, and how to get rid of it. You have seen some of the common mistakes and dangers, and have, hopefully, developed a serious respect for the power and the potential for problems that pointers represent.

LESSON 14
Testing

In this lesson you will make a few changes to the calculator and then per-form some testing. You will learn about C++ program testing strategies and use them. You will also learn about a few miscellaneous language features.

Why Storage from the Heap Makes Testing Critical

Every program should be tested every time it is changed. But as you saw in the last lesson, when you start using heap-allocated storage and point-ers, the danger of a problem arising when the program runs (at runtime) is much greater. Just look at some of the errors you might encounter:

- Uninitialized pointer

- Pointer initialized to NULL

- Deleting twice

- Not deleting at all

- Going past the bounds of an array

These problems may or may not have consequences anywhere near the place where the error occurred. They may, like the fourth error listed here, not have any apparent effect at all.

C++ compilers enforce good programming practices such as strong typ-ing, but still allow many dangerous errors to occur. There are strategies for building more testable programs, but keep in mind that no amount of testing will uncover *all* problems.

Making the Calculator More General with a "Little Language"

You need to make a little change to the *user interface* of the calculator, to make it more "testable."

 User Interface The part of the program that sends output to the user and gets input from the user.

Instead of prompting users to input numbers or indicate that they want to stop, the program will now get commands from a "little language." These commands will be typed into the running program when it needs input—just as you type on your handheld calculator.

A statement in this language has the following form:

`<operator><operand>`

`<operator>` can be any of the following:

+ to add the operand to the accumulator

- to subtract the operand from the accumulator

* to multiply the accumulator by the operand

/ to divide the accumulator by the operand

@ to set the accumulator to a specific value

= to show the current value in the accumulator

? to show the tape

! to have the calculator test itself

. to stop the program

An entire set of operators and operands can be entered on a single line (for example, +3-2*12/3=, which outputs 4). Note that our little language has no precedence and performs its steps strictly from left to right (0+3 = 3; 3-2 = 1; 1*12 = 12; 12/3 = 4).

An operand is optional for the =, ?, !, and . operators.

Changes to `main()`

The `main()` function has a few changes, as shown in Listing 14.1.

LISTING 14.1   `main()` with Changes

```
 1: int main(int argc, char* argv[])
 2: {
 3:     SAMSErrorHandling::Initialize();
 4:
*5:     char Operator; // Used in the loop
 6:
 7:     do
 8:     {
 9:         try
10:         {
11:             Operator = GetOperator();
12:
*13:             if
*14:             (
*15:                 Operator == '+' ||
*16:                 Operator == '-' ||
*17:                 Operator == '*' ||
*18:                 Operator == '/' ||
*19:                 Operator == '@' // Set value
*20:             )
*21:             {
22:                 float Operand = GetOperand();
23:                 Accumulator(Operator,Operand);
24:             }
*25:             else if (Operator == '!')
*26:             {
*27:                 SelfTest();
*28:             }
*29:             else if (Operator == '.')
*30:             {
*31:                 // Do nothing, we are stopping
```

LISTING 14.1 Continued

```
*32:            }
*33:            else // Some other operator, no operand
*34:            {
*35:                Accumulator(Operator);
*36:            };
 37:        }
 38:        catch (runtime_error RuntimeError)
 39:        {
 40:            SAMSErrorHandling::HandleRuntimeError
                  ➥(RuntimeError);
 41:        }
 42:        catch (...)
 43:        {
 44:            SAMSErrorHandling::HandleNotANumberError();
 45:        };
 46:    }
*47:    while (Operator != '.'); // Continue
 48:
 49:    Tape('.'); // Tell the tape we are terminating
 50:
 51:    return 0;
 52: }
```

ANALYSIS Line 5 moves the variable Operator outside the loop because its value will be used to stop the loop, as seen in line 47.

Lines 13–21 identify and get the operands for operators that have them, and then give them to the accumulator.

You can see that the name of the Accumulate() function has been changed to Accumulator(). Naming a function with a noun instead of a verb indicates that it has an internal state and that it does not depend solely on the arguments passed in any specific call.

Lines 25–28 run the self-test.

Line 29 makes sure that the program does nothing when the . operator is entered. The empty block makes this clear.

Lines 33–36 are for any operator with no operand. This call on the Accumulator() has only one parameter.

Accumulator() Changes

The Accumulator() shown in Listing 14.2 has some new lines in its
switch statement, because a much smaller percentage of its operators are
recorded on the Tape().

LISTING 14.2   Accumulator() Implementing New Operators

```
 *1: float Accumulator
        ↪(const char theOperator,const float theOperand = 0)
  2: {
  3:     static float myAccumulator = 0;
  4:
  5:     switch (theOperator)
  6:     {
  7:        case '+':
  8:
  9:            myAccumulator = myAccumulator + theOperand;
*10:            Tape(theOperator,theOperand);
 11:            break;
 12:
 13:        case '-':
 14:
 15:            myAccumulator = myAccumulator - theOperand;
*16:            Tape(theOperator,theOperand);
 17:            break;
 18:
 19:        case '*':
 20:
 21:            myAccumulator = myAccumulator,theOperand;
*22:            Tape(theOperator,theOperand);
 23:            break;
 24:
 25:        case '/':
 26:
 27:            myAccumulator = myAccumulator / theOperand;
*28:            Tape(theOperator,theOperand);
 29:            break;
 30:
*31:        case '@':
*32:
*33:            myAccumulator = theOperand;
*34:            Tape(theOperator,theOperand);
```

LISTING 14.2 Continued

```
*35:            break;
 36:
*37:        case '=':
*38:            cout << endl << myAccumulator << endl;
*39:            break;
 40:
 41:        case '?':  // Display the tape
 42:            Tape(theOperator);
 43:            break;
 44:
 45:        default:
 46:            throw
 47:                runtime_error
 48:                    ("Error - Invalid operator");
 49:    };
 50:
*51:    return myAccumulator;
 52: }
```

ANALYSIS Line 1 has one of the most substantial changes. It now has the Accumulator() returning the current value of myAccumulator on line 51.

There is a new feature shown in the formal argument theOperand on line 1. An equal sign and a zero follow the formal argument name. This means that the formal argument is an *optional* argument, and if the actual argument is not provided in a function call, the argument will be given a default value—in this case 0. The default value lets the compiler know that the call in line 49 of main() is allowed.

The other new lines are straightforward—they simply add calls to Tape() for every operator whose action is to be recorded, or implement new operators, such as setting the accumulator value on lines 31–35 and displaying the accumulator value on lines 37–39.

The Input Function Changes

Getting the operator and operand requires a minor change—as you can see in Listing 14.3, the prompt has been removed.

LISTING 14.3   GetOperator() and GetOperand() Without the Prompt

```
 1: char GetOperator(void)
 2: {
 3:     char Operator;
 4:     cin >> Operator;
 5:
 6:     return Operator;
 7: }
 8:
 9: float GetOperand(void)
10: {
11:     float Operand;
12:     cin >> Operand;
13:
14:     return Operand;
15: }
```

The SelfTest Function

The SelfTest function (see Listing 14.4) is performed by line 27 of main() when you enter ! as input. It runs a test of the accumulator.

LISTING 14.4   SelfTest()

```
 1: void SelfTest(void)
 2: {
 3:     float OldValue = Accumulator('=');
 4:
 5:     try
 6:     {
 7:         if
 8:         (
 9:             TestOK('@',0,0) &&
10:             TestOK('+',3,3) &&
11:             TestOK('-',2,1) &&
12:             TestOK('*',4,4) &&
13:             TestOK('/',2,2)
14:         )
15:         {
16:             cout << "Test completed successfully." << endl;
17:         }
18:         else
19:         {
```

LISTING 14.4 Continued

```
20:                cout << "Test failed." << endl;
21:           };
22:      }
23:      catch (...)
24:      {
25:           cout <<
                    "An exception occured during self test." <<
                    endl;
26:      };
27:
28:      Accumulator('@',OldValue);
29: }
```

ANALYSIS This function is wrapped in a try/catch, so if the test encounters a problem that throws an exception, the function can restore things to the state they were in before the test started. It may also catch errors resulting from the use of heap allocation in Tape(). But remember that heap allocation errors can do so much damage that an exception may never be thrown.

Line 3 saves the value of the accumulator, which is restored in Line 28.

Lines 7–14 actually execute the tests. This block tests every operator that changes the accumulator by calling the TestOK() function. Because this uses the relational operator &&, if any tests fail, the self-test fails.

The TestOK() Function

SelfTest() uses TestOK() (see Listing 14.5) to determine whether each operator/operand submitted to the Accumulator() provides the expected result.

LISTING 14.5 TestOK()

```
1: bool TestOK
2: (
3:      const char theOperator,
4:      const float theOperand,
5:      const float theExpectedResult
6: )
7: {
```

LISTING 14.5 Continued

```
 8:     float Result = Accumulator(theOperator,theOperand);
 9:
10:     if (Result == theExpectedResult)
11:     {
12:         cout << theOperator << theOperand <<
            ➡" - succeeded." << endl;
13:         return true;
14:     }
15:     else
16:     {
17:         cout <<
18:             theOperator << theOperand << " - failed. " <<
19:             "Expected " << theExpectedResult <<
            ➡", got " << result <<
20:             endl;
21:
22:         return false;
23:     };
24: }
```

This is a function that has a bool result and three const arguments—the operator, the operand, and the result expected from the accumulator. The function performs the operation and reports whether or not the result matches what is expected.

Test functions like this and SelfTest() *must* be kept simple. You need to be able to validate test functions by eye (by performing what is called a *walkthrough*). If they are wrong, you might hunt for bugs (runtime errors) that don't exist or miss ones that do.

A Slight Change to the Tape()

You only need to change one line in the Tape() function to aid testing.

Convert

```
*3:     static const int myTapeChunk = 20;
```

to

```
*3:     static const int myTapeChunk = 3;
```

Why? To verify that heap allocations are working, testing must provoke `Tape()` to resize the tape at least once. This is done by making the chunk size smaller than the number of operations in the test.

Running the Program

It's time to look for errors. Let's run a self-test:

OUTPUT

```
1: !
2:
3: 0
4: @0 - succeeded.
5: +3 - succeeded.
6: -2 - succeeded.
7: *4 - failed. Expected 4, got 1
8: Test failed.
```

Test line 1 shows the self-test operator being input to the program—type it and press Enter. Line 3 shows the value of the accumulator being saved by the test, as a result of line 3 in `SelfTest()`. The tests succeed until output line 7.

Notice that only three of the four tests have run. Why didn't the division test run?

Short-circuit Evaluation

One of the nice things about the `&&` relational operator is that it uses what is called *short-circuit evaluation*. This means that as soon as any expression connected by `&&` is `false`, subsequent expressions will not be executed. And why should they? As soon as any expression is `false`, the entire expression will be `false`.

Further tests are not performed if any of them fail, because each test's expected result requires a correct result from the prior test. But short-circuit evaluation can be a problem if you expect a function in such an expression to execute regardless of the outcome of prior expressions.

What Was Wrong?

Fortunately, the self-test points you right to the error line:

```
19:         case '*':
20:
21:             myAccumulator = myAccumulator,theOperand;
```

You will notice that the program is not multiplying in line 21. Instead of a
*, there is a ,. This was not a contrived error. I actually made this error
while writing the example and discovered it in the self-test.

You might wonder why the compiler lets you make this mistake. It turns
out that the , is the infix *comma operator*. It returns the value of the right-
most operand as its result. There are some uses for this, but it is very
uncommon.

Fix the Error and Rerun

Once you've fixed the error and rerun the program, you will see that the
program works fine. Even the Tape() reallocations seem to have no problem. But be skeptical. Heap allocation errors can hide in even the best
code and not show up in testing.

Debugging Without a Debugger

If you have an Integrated Development Environment (IDE), you have a
debugger—a special program that lets you see the program lines as they
execute and examine values. It may even catch exceptions and take you to
the exception line. But if you don't have a debugger, the strategies discussed in the following sections may help you find the cause of runtime
errors.

Wolf Fencing

Imagine a farmer who has a wolf on his property, howling every night. To
catch the wolf, the farmer builds an unclimbable fence around and across
the middle of his property, and then listens for the howling. It will be on
one side or the other of the fence. He then goes to that side of the fence

and splits that half of the property with another fence and then listens again. He repeats the process until he has a little fence enclosure with a wolf inside it.

Runtime errors (bugs) are like the wolf. They cry out, but it is sometimes difficult to pin down exactly where they live. Determine the general area of the problem and at the top and bottom of that area, display critical values that represent what is going wrong—perhaps the content of a variable. If the value is okay at the top and bad at the bottom, put the same display somewhere in the middle. Repeat the dividing process until you find the error.

Printing Values

You have used cout and cerr to display values. Later you will see that you can use a file on disk as the destination of output, which can be an even better method of finding complex errors.

Using #defines to Turn Debugging On and Off

#ifdef, #define, and #endif allow you to avoid including a header more than once. You can also use the preprocessor commands #define, #ifdef (a new command that means "if defined"), and #endif to allow code to be seen by the compiler only when a particular symbol has been defined. For instance:

```
#define DEBUGGING
...
#ifdef DEBUGGING
    cout << "Starting debug - value = " << SomeValue << endl;
#endif
```

In this code, the symbol DEBUGGING is defined (perhaps at the top of a program, or even in an include file). If the symbol is defined, the cout will be compiled, and the program will display SomeValue.

The nice thing about this is that debug lines using the #ifdef DEBUGGING will not be compiled and will have no effect if you remove the #define.

This reduces the risk that you might damage the program by removing debug statements with the editor.

Summing Up

You have seen how to make the calculator use a little language as its user interface, how to give it the capability to test itself, and how to find an error when it is reported by the self-test. You have also learned some strategies for debugging your program, even when the only tools you have are a compiler and an editor.

Lesson 15
Structures and Types

In this lesson, you'll learn about creating sets of named constants that are related to each other, creating data structures that can hold many different variables in a single container, and calling functions through pointers.

Getting Organized

By now, you have probably noticed the rhythm of development: add features, develop features, refactor, retest, and repeat. It is time once again to shift things around in the example.

Figure 15.1 shows the new organization. `Accumulator()`, `Tape()`, and the parts of `main()` that interact with the user have each been moved into their own modules. These three modules are all in the `SAMSCalculator` namespace.

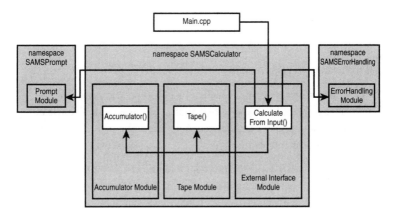

Figure 15.1 A new arrangement of modules.

The arrows show how the functions call each other. main() calls CalculateFromInput(), which calls Accumulator() and Tape(). main() can also call functions in the other modules.

After this reorganization, it is time to move on to a very powerful feature of C++: the capability to create new data types.

You have used "built-in" types such as char, int, and float. Each of these types carries some restrictions. char can only be used for characters, int for numbers without decimal places, and float for any numbers. When you create a new type, you can also have the compiler produce an error when a variable of this type is used incorrectly.

Declaring Enumerated Types

An *enumerated type* is a data type whose variables can only take on a value from the set of constants listed in the type declaration (*enumerated* means "named one by one"). For instance, you can declare an enumerated type anOperator, and you can offer six possible values for it: add, subtract, multiply, divide, reset, and query (these are just like the Accumulator() operators).

The syntax for enumerated types is

```
enum{constantname,constantname...};
```

Here's an example:

```
enum anOperator {add,subtract,multiply,divide,reset,query};
```

This statement has two purposes:

1. It makes anOperator the name of a new type, and restricts it to having one of the six specified values, just as an int is restricted to having numbers without decimal places. You can later define variables of anOperator type.

2. It makes add a symbolic constant with the value 0, subtract a symbolic constant with the value 1, multiply a symbolic constant with the value 2, and so forth. Every symbolic constant in the enumerated type has a value that is, underneath, a number. If

you don't specify otherwise, each constant will by definition have the value of its position in the list minus 1 (this is just like array element numbering, where the first element is 0, the second is 1, and so on).

You can now define and use a variable of your new type:

```
1: enum anOperator {add,subtract,multiply,divide,reset,query};
2: anOperator Operator;
3: Operator = '+'; // Will produce a compiler error message
4: Operator = add; // Will compile successfully
```

ANALYSIS Line 1 is the declaration of the new type. The type name is prefixed with "an." Using the "a" or "an" prefix makes it easy to tell that you are working with a user-defined type, as opposed to a standard type, a local variable or constant, a formal argument, or a static local variable.

Line 2 defines a variable of this new type. Line 3 fails to compile because it attempts to assign something other than one of the enumerated constants to the variable, while line 4 compiles successfully because it does assign an enumerated constant to the variable.

Using Enumerations in `Accumulator()`

The `AccumulatorModule` header file shown in Listing 15.1 declares an enumeration.

LISTING 15.1   Enumerations in the `AccumulatorModule` Header

```
 1: #ifndef AccumulatorModuleH
 2: #define AccumulatorModuleH
 3:
 4: namespace SAMSCalculator
 5: {
*6:     enum anOperator
*7:         {add,subtract,multiply,divide,reset,query};
 8:
 9:     float Accumulator
10:     (
*11:         const anOperator theOperator,
```

LISTING 15.1   Continued

```
12:          const float theOperand = 0
13:      );
14: };
15:
16: #endif
```

ANALYSIS Lines 6 and 7 declare the enum type (and because it is in this module's header file, any user of the module can now define variables of the type). Line 11 indicates that you are required to pass an argument of the enumerated type as theOperator to the Accumulator()— you can no longer pass a character. This makes the Accumulator() safer, because the compiler will protect it against invalid operators.

The implementation has not changed much, except that everything pertaining to Tape() has been removed to ExternalInterfaceModule functions, and it now uses the enumeration constants for switch statement cases. The updated program appears in Listing 15.2.

LISTING 15.2   Enumerations in the AccumulatorModule Implementation

```
 1: #include <exception>
 2: #include <ios>
 3:
 4: #include "AccumulatorModule.h"
 5:
 6: namespace SAMSCalculator
 7: {
 8:     using namespace std;
 9:
10:     float Accumulator
11:     (
12:         const anOperator theOperator,
13:         const float theOperand
14:     )
15:     {
16:         static float myAccumulator = 0;
17:
18:         switch (theOperator)
19:         {
```

LISTING 15.2 Continued

```
20:              case add:
21:                  myAccumulator = myAccumulator + theOperand;
22:                  break;
23:
24:              case subtract:
25:                  myAccumulator = myAccumulator - theOperand;
26:                  break;
27:
28:              case multiply:
29:                  myAccumulator = myAccumulator * theOperand;
30:                  break;
31:
32:              case divide:
33:                  myAccumulator = myAccumulator / theOperand;
34:                  break;
35:
36:              case reset:
37:                  myAccumulator = theOperand;
38:                  break;
39:
40:              case query:
41:                  // We always return the result - do nothing
42:                  break;
43:
44:              default:
45:                  throw
*46:                      runtime_error
47:                          ("Error - Invalid operator");
48:          };
49:
50:          return myAccumulator;
51:      };
52: };
```

Note that line 44 contains the default case. This line probably won't ever be executed now that the compiler checks the correctness of theOperand. But if you were maintaining this program and accidentally deleted, say, line 40, control would flow to the default case and you would be notified of the problem. It is always best to leave the default case, even if you never need it.

Declaring Structure Types

Enumeration types are useful, but there are more powerful types you can declare, called *structure types.*

Structure types let you bundle up a set of *member variables* into a single variable. Then you can keep related data together in a single package and pass it around just as you pass an `int` or a `char`. You can even make an array of structures.

A structure type is declared with keyword `struct`, a name, and any number of typed members:

```
struct typename
{
    type membervariablename...
};
```

Here's an example:

```
struct aTapeElement
{
    char Operator;
    float Operand;
};
```

Structures on the Stack

You can declare a variable of a structure type on the stack. For instance:

```
aTapeElement TapeElement;
```

But how do you initialize it? This is where the C++ *member selection* (`.`) operator comes in. It allows you to get or set the member variable values:

```
TapeElement.Operator = '+';
TapeElement.Operand = 234;
char Operator = TapeElement.Operator;
```

You can see that a well-chosen structure variable name makes this read more clearly.

It is also possible to create arrays of structures:

```
aTapeElement TapeElement[20];
```

This enables you to select member variables from any element:

```
TapeElement[5].Operator = '+';
TapeElement[5].Operand = 234;
```

Structures from the Heap

Structures are also frequently created with new. For instance:

```
aTapeElement *TapeElement = new aTapeElement;
```

This reads, "define a pointer to aTapeElement called TapeElement and initialize it with the location of the space created on the heap by new, with that space being the size of aTapeElement."

You can use the period to select the member variables, but you must dereference the pointer first:

```
(*TapeElement).Operator = '+';
(*TapeElement).Operand = 234;
```

Because this is so frequently needed, C++ offers a shorthand for this expression, the *pointer member selection* (->) operator.

```
TapeElement->Operator = '+';
TapeElement->Operand = 234;
```

Naturally, you must always remember to delete a heap-allocated structure, but this is done in the same way for structure types as for simple types:

```
delete TapeElement;
```

You can create an array of structures on the heap with

```
aTapeElement *TapeElement = new TapeElement[10];
```

This still allows you to use the member selection operator in a normal fashion:

```
TapeElement[5].Operand = 234;
```

And you delete it normally as well:

```
delete [] TapeElement;
```

A Unidirectional Linked List with Structures for the Tape

One of the interesting capabilities offered by allocating structures from the heap is that you can use a pointer in the structure to link structures together into a list (called a *linked list*). For instance, you can create an indefinitely long list of aTapeElement structures by adding a member variable to aTapeElement that is a pointer to the next aTapeElement:

```
struct aTapeElement
{
    char Operator;
    float Operand;
    aTapeElement *NextElement;
};
```

Then you can link them together, like this:

```
1: aTapeElement Tape;
2: aTapeElement SecondElement = new aTapeElement;
3: Tape.NextElement = SecondElement;
4: aTapeElement ThirdElement = new aTapeElement;
5: Tape.NextElement->NextElement = ThirdElement;
```

Line 5 uses the pointer member selection operator to get to the second element's NextElement member and add the ThirdElement.

Let's look at this in the revised Tape() that appears in Listing 15.3.

LISTING 15.3   Structures in Tape()

```
 1: void Tape
 2:     (const char theOperator,const float theOperand)
 3: {
 4:     static aTapeElement *TapeRoot = NULL;
 5:
 6:     if (theOperator == '?') // Print the tape
 7:     {
 8:         PrintTape(TapeRoot);
 9:     }
10:     else if (theOperator == '.') // Program is stopping
11:     {
12:         DeleteTape(TapeRoot);
```

LISTING 15.3 Continued

```
 13:    }
 14:    else // Normal operation: Add to the tape
 15:    {
*16:        aTapeElement *NewElement = new aTapeElement;
 17:
*18:        NewElement->Operator = theOperator;
*19:        NewElement->Operand = theOperand;
*20:        NewElement->NextElement = NULL;
 21:
*22:        if (TapeRoot == NULL)
 23:        {
*24:            // This is the first Element
*25:            TapeRoot = NewElement;
 26:        }
 27:        else
 28:        {
 29:            // Add the Element to the end of the
 30:            // last Element in the list
 31:
 32:            // Start at the beginning...
*33:            aTapeElement *CurrentTapeElement = TapeRoot;
 34:
 35:            // ...skip to the end
*36:            while
*37:                (
*38:                    CurrentTapeElement->NextElement != NULL
*39:                )
 40:            {
*41:                CurrentTapeElement =
*42:                    CurrentTapeElement->NextElement;
 43:            };
*44:
 45:            // CurrentTapeElement is the last Element
 46:            // Add to it...
*47:            CurrentTapeElement->NextElement = NewElement;
 48:        };
 49:    };
 50: };
```

ANALYSIS Lines 16–47 add to the tape. You can see that the logic has become simpler. You don't have to do array reallocation and copying. In fact, there is no longer any need to check whether the tape is full, because the code can always add a new element and has no limit.

Line 16 creates the new tape element. Lines 18–20 set its member variables using the pointer member selector. Note that the `NextElement` member is set to `NULL`, which means "points to nothing."

Line 22 checks to see whether there are any elements in the tape yet—when `TapeRoot` is `NULL`, the new element is the first and its location is assigned to `TapeRoot`.

Lines 33–43 are performed when there are already one or more elements in the tape. The loop scans the list and stops at the last element, which is the only one with a `NULL` `NextElement`.

Line 47 sets the last element's `NextElement` pointer to point to the new element. Now the new element is the last one.

Function Pointers and Callbacks

Data on the stack has a location—also called an *address*. So does data on the heap. And so does every line of code in your program. In fact, when you read about "the flow of control," you should actually think of a variable used by the operating system to keep track of which instruction of the program is being performed. Top-to-bottom control flow is just like moving through an array using an index or pointer.

In fact, a program to run programs might look something like Listing 15.4.

LISTING 15.4   Outline of a Program to Run Programs

```
1: struct anInstruction
2: {
3:     anInstructionCode InstructionCode;
4:     anInstruction *NextInstruction;
5: };
6:
7: anInstruction *Program =
8:     new anInstruction[NumberOfInstructions];
9:
10: anInstruction *CurrentInstruction = Program;
11:
```

LISTING 15.4 Continued

```
12: do
13: {
14:     Perform(CurrentInstruction.InstructionCode);
15:
16:     CurrentInstruction =
17:         CurrentInstruction.NextInstruction;
18: }
19: while (CurrentInstruction != NULL);
```

Because anInstruction contains a pointer to the next instruction, this program can even offer the equivalent of if statements and function calls. Figure 15.2 shows a "flow of control" that is just like a C++ function call.

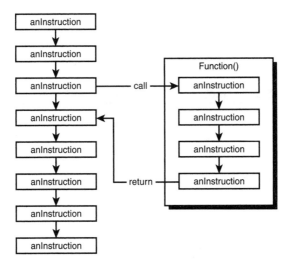

FIGURE 15.2 Control flow through pointers.

C++ allows you to get the address of a function and use it for a function call in a very similar way—through a *function pointer*. Function pointers, like other pointers, are typed. Here are some examples of declaring them:

```
typedef char (*ToGetAnOperator)(void);
typedef float (*ToGetAnOperand)(void);
typedef void (*ToHandleResults)(const float theResult);
typedef void (*ToDisplayMessage)(const char *theMessage);
```

Unlike other type declarations, function pointer declarations require the typedef keyword. Other than that, the only difference between a function pointer declaration and a function prototype is that the name of the function is replaced by (*nameoftype). * means "pointer to function of type named nameoftype" in this context.

You can declare variables of these types. Have a look at a structure declaration with function pointer members:

```
struct aCalculatorExternalInterface
{
    ToGetAnOperator GetAnOperator;
    ToGetAnOperand GetAnOperand;
    ToHandleResults HandleResults;
    ToDisplayMessage DisplayMessage;
};
```

But how can you assign to these members? The new main.cpp in Listing 15.5 shows such assignment in action.

LISTING 15.5   Function Pointer Assignment in main.cpp

```
 1: char GetOperator(void)
 2: {
 3:     char Operator;
 4:     cin >> Operator;
 5:
 6:     return Operator;
 7: }
 8:
 9: float GetOperand(void)
10: {
11:     float Operand;
12:     cin >> Operand;
13:
14:     return Operand;
15: }
16:
17: void DisplayValueOnConsole(float theValue)
18: {
19:     cout << endl << theValue << endl;
20: }
21:
```

LISTING 15.5 Continued

```
22: void DisplayMessageOnConsole(const char *theMessage)
23: {
24:     cout << theMessage << endl;
25: }
26:
27: int main(int argc, char* argv[])
28: {
29:     SAMSCalculator::aCalculatorExternalInterface
30:         CalculatorExternalInterface;
31:
*32:    CalculatorExternalInterface.GetAnOperator =
*33:        GetOperator;
*34:
*35:    CalculatorExternalInterface.GetAnOperand =
*36:        GetOperand;
*37:
*38:    CalculatorExternalInterface.HandleResults =
*39:        DisplayValueOnConsole;
*40:
*41:    CalculatorExternalInterface.DisplayMessage =
*42:        DisplayMessageOnConsole;
43:
44:     return SAMSCalculator::CalculateFromInput
45:         (CalculatorExternalInterface);
46: }
```

ANALYSIS Lines 32–42 assign the addresses of the functions to the member variable function pointers. You can tell that this is assignment rather than calling because the functions don't have parentheses or arguments at the end.

Calling a Function from a Pointer

You're using this structure and its function pointers to create a special kind of programming pattern known as a *callback*. A callback occurs when one module supplies another module with pointers to some of its functions so that the other module can call those functions. In this case, you are doing this so that the CalculateFromInput() function can use main.cpp's input and output functions without knowing anything about main.cpp.

Let's look at some selected lines from the function NextCalculation() in Listing 15.6. NextCalculation() is called by CalculateFromInput() to implement the loop that used to be the core of main().

LISTING 15.6 Calling Through Function Pointers Seen in Excerpts from NextCalculation()

```
 1:    bool NextCalculation
 2:    (
 3:        const aCalculatorExternalInterface
            ➥&theCalculatorExternalInterface
 4:    )
 5:    {
*6:        char Operator =
            ➥theCalculatorExternalInterface.GetAnOperator();
30:            if (OperatorValue == query)
31:            {
*32:                theCalculatorExternalInterface.
                    ➥HandleResults(Result);
33:            };

38:            case '+': case '-': case '*': case '/':
39:            {
*40:                int Number =
                    ➥theCalculatorExternalInterface.
                    ➥GetAnOperand();
```

ANALYSIS Line 6 shows a call through the function pointer GetAnOperator to the main.cpp function GetOperator(). Line 32 shows a call through HandleResults to DisplayValueOnConsole(). And line 40 shows a call to main.cpp's GetOperand() through GetAnOperand.

Note that these lines are broken on the member selection operator (.). Though the compiler allows it, you should normally avoid breaking lines in this way.

Also notable is the formal argument to NextCalculation, which is a reference to aCalculatorExternalInterface type structure. You should always pass structures by reference. If you don't, the program will make a

copy of the actual argument (which is time-consuming), give it to the
function (also time-consuming), and make any structural changes to the
copy, not to the original.

Summing Up

Enumerated types, structure types, and function pointer types offer
tremendous power for creating advanced programs. You have seen how to
declare them, define variables of the new types, use constants from the
enumerations, select members from structures, and assign and call
through function pointers. All of this will help get you ready for object-
oriented classes. But first, you can take a break from the hard stuff and
look at reading and writing files on disk.

LESSON 16
File I/O

In this lesson, you will learn about reading and writing disk files and saving and restoring the state of a program.

Saving the Tape Between Sessions

So far, all of the calculator's actions have been based on your input, and when you stop the calculator, all of the work you've entered into it has been lost. This is because program variables only retain their content while the program is running. Their collected content is often referred to as the program's *state*.

Most computers have a file system, whose purpose is to retain data between program runs. And every programming language has a way to put data into files in the file system and get data from them. C++ uses a special kind of stream—the fstream (file stream), which is similar to cin and cout—for that purpose.

fstreams

Unlike cin and cout, the file stream #include<fstream> does not provide variables representing files. Instead, you must define a file stream variable of type ifstream (input file stream) or ofstream (output file stream) in your program and then open it with the *fstreamvariable*.open() function. You have to provide the path to locate the file within the operating system's file system as the argument to open(). Consult your operating system documentation for the correct way to specify such paths.

If you only specify a filename without other information, it is usually assumed that the file is in the same place as your program.

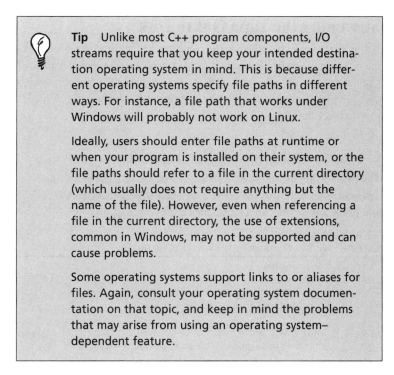

Tip Unlike most C++ program components, I/O streams require that you keep your intended destination operating system in mind. This is because different operating systems specify file paths in different ways. For instance, a file path that works under Windows will probably not work on Linux.

Ideally, users should enter file paths at runtime or when your program is installed on their system, or the file paths should refer to a file in the current directory (which usually does not require anything but the name of the file). However, even when referencing a file in the current directory, the use of extensions, common in Windows, may not be supported and can cause problems.

Some operating systems support links to or aliases for files. Again, consult your operating system documentation on that topic, and keep in mind the problems that may arise from using an operating system–dependent feature.

You can use an input or output stream variable in the same way as cin and cout. Use the extractor (>>) and inserter (<<) operators to get or put data.

When finished, you may need to close the stream with close(), though if the stream variable is declared on the stack, the stream will be closed automatically when it goes *out of scope*.

Scope The lifetime of a variable. Most variable scope lasts while control flows within the block where the variable is defined (not counting function calls). The scope of global and static variables is the entire program, though they are only usable (often called *visible*) within their defining module or function, respectively.

Streaming the Tape Out to Disk

If you want to save the work you've done during the calculator session, the natural place to begin is with Tape(). Tape() contains every command you entered into the calculator, and, if saved to disk at the end of a session and then read back in at the beginning of the next session, it can be used to redo everything you did previously.

Opening and Closing the Tape File

The new version of TapeModule shown in Listing 16.1 has a function called StreamTape(), which opens a tape output stream, writes the content of the tape to that stream, and then closes the stream.

LISTING 16.1   StreamTape() in TapeModule

```
 1: void StreamTape
 2: (
 3:     const char *theTapeOutputStreamName,
 4:     aTapeElement *theTapeRoot
 5: )
 6: {
*7:     if (theTapeOutputStreamName == NULL) return;
 8:
*9:     ofstream TapeOutputStream;
10:
11:     try
12:     {
*13:         TapeOutputStream.exceptions
*14:             (TapeOutputStream.failbit);
15:
*16:         TapeOutputStream.open
*17:             (theTapeOutputStreamName,ios_base::out);
18:
*19:         aTapeElement *CurrentTapeElement = theTapeRoot;
20:
*21:         while (CurrentTapeElement != NULL)
22:         {
*23:             TapeOutputStream <<
*24:                 CurrentTapeElement->Operator <<
*25:                 CurrentTapeElement->Operand;
26:
*27:             CurrentTapeElement =
```

LISTING 16.1   Continued

```
*28:                CurrentTapeElement->NextElement;
 29:          };
 30:
*31:          TapeOutputStream.close();
 32:      }
*33:      catch (ios_base::failure &IOError)
*34:      {
*35:          SAMSErrorHandling::HandleOutputStreamError
*36:              (TapeOutputStream,IOError);
*37:      };
 38: }
```

> **ANALYSIS**   Line 7 protects the function against the possibility that no filename has been provided. If no filename is provided, the tape is not streamed to a file.

Line 9 defines the output file stream type (ofstream) variable.

Lines 13–14 and 33–37 are dedicated to protecting the program against any problem with the file stream—for instance, an invalid filename—by catching any exception.

Line 13 sets up the stream variable to throw exceptions, just as you did for cin in the ErrorHandlingModule.

Line 16 opens the stream using the provided name. It tells the open() function that the ios_base::out enumerated type constant should be used to open the file for output. If the file fails to open, an exception may be thrown, which will be caught in the exception-handling catch on line 33. When a stream is opened with ios_base::out, anything already in the file is wiped out, so this starts the program with an empty file for the current tape.

Line 19 begins the loop that will scan the tape, starting with the root element. Line 21 checks whether there are any elements in the tape and performs the loop as long as there are more elements.

Lines 23–25 use the familiar inserter operator (<<) to write out the operator and operand from the element to the file.

Line 27 moves to the next tape element and the loop will repeat as long as that NextElement pointer is not NULL.

Line 31 closes the stream. However, this line is not strictly necessary. When control flows out of the block, the stream variable goes out of scope, which causes the stream to be automatically closed.

Changes to Make `StreamTape()` Work

The `Tape()` function needs a new argument so it can give the filename to the `StreamTape()` function. Here's the new prototype:

```
void Tape
(
    const char theOperator,
    const float theOperand = 0,
    const char *theTapeOutputStreamName = NULL
);
```

You can see that the new argument and its default value are last. Giving the new argument a default value ensures that it will not be required in every call to `Tape()`, so you won't have to change every call to `Tape()`, just the one that supplies the name.

Inside `Tape()`, `StreamTape()` is called just before `DeleteTape()`.

Providing the Tape Filename

The tape file path will be brought in from the outside—but not through `cin`. Instead, the arguments to `main()` are the source. `argv` contains an element for each of the words on the command line. The zeroth word is the program name. So the first word can be the name of the tape file. Here's the changed line in `main()` to pass this to `Tape()`:

```
SAMSCalculator::Tape('.',0,argv[1]);
```

Note that `argv` stands for "argument value."

Recalling the Tape

If you run the program and open the resulting tape file, you'll see exactly what you entered during your session. The next stage is to get the calculator to read in the tape at startup and perform those commands as if you had typed them.

main.cpp is the only module affected by this next stage.

Replaying the Tape to Restore State

The GetOperator() and GetOperand() functions in main.cpp can first get input from the saved tape. When that runs out, they can then get input from cin instead. Listing 16.2 shows how this works.

LISTING 16.2   main.cpp Reading the Tape from a File

```
 1: #include <iostream>
 2: #include <ios>
 3: #include <fstream>
 4:
 5: #include "PromptModule.h"
 6: #include "ErrorHandlingModule.h"
 7: #include "AccumulatorModule.h"
 8: #include "TapeModule.h"
 9: #include "ExternalInterfaceModule.h"
10:
11: using namespace std;
12:
*13: ifstream TapeInputStream; // Global variable for callback
14:
15: char GetOperator(void)
16: {
17:     char Operator;
18:
19:     if
20:         (
*21:             TapeInputStream.is_open() &&
*22:             (!TapeInputStream.eof())
23:         )
24:     {
*25:         TapeInputStream >> Operator;
26:     }
27:     else
28:     {
*29:         cin >> Operator;
30:     };
31:
```

LISTING 16.2   Continued

```
32:     return Operator;
33: }
34:
35: float GetOperand(void)
36: {
37:     float Operand = 1;
38:
*39:     if
*40:         (
*41:             TapeInputStream.is_open() &&
*42:             (!TapeInputStream.eof())
*43:         )
*44:     {
*45:         TapeInputStream >> Operand;
*46:     }
*47:     else
*48:     {
*49:         cin >> Operand;
*50:     };
51:
52:     return Operand;
53: }
54:
55: void DisplayValueOnConsole(float theValue)
56: {
57:     cout << endl << theValue << endl;
58: }
59:
60: int main(int argc, char* argv[])
61: {
62:     SAMSErrorHandling::Initialize();
63:
*64:     if (argc > 1) // A filename is present
*65:     {
*66:         try
*67:         {
*68:             TapeInputStream.exceptions(cin.failbit);
*69:             TapeInputStream.open(argv[1],ios_base::in);
*70:         }
*71:         catch (ios_base::failure &IOError)
*72:         {
*73:             SAMSErrorHandling::HandleInputStreamError
*74:                 (TapeInputStream,IOError);
*75:             // The stream will be unopened
```

LISTING 16.2   Continued

```
*76:                 // but the failure bits will not be set
*77:        };
*78:
*79:    }; // otherwise, the stream exists
*80:           // but is closed and cannot be used;
 81:
 82:    SAMSCalculator::aCalculatorExternalInterface
 83:        CalculatorExternalInterface;
 84:
 85:    CalculatorExternalInterface.GetAnOperator =
 86:        GetOperator;
 87:
 88:    CalculatorExternalInterface.GetAnOperand =
 89:        GetOperand;
 90:
 91:    CalculatorExternalInterface.HandleResults =
 92:        DisplayValueOnConsole;
 93:
 94:    int Result = SAMSCalculator::CalculateFromInput
 95:        (CalculatorExternalInterface);
 96:
 97:    // Don't leave the file open, because otherwise Tape()
 98:    // will not be able to stream the current session
*99:    TapeInputStream.close();
100:
101:    // Stream and delete the tape
*102:   SAMSCalculator::Tape('.',0,argv[1]);
103:
104:    return Result;
105: }
```

ANALYSIS   Line 13 is a module-level global variable (other modules cannot use this variable) that defines the TapeInputStream. By
making this a global variable, you can avoid passing the stream into the
CalculateFromInput() function, confining this set of changes to the
main.cpp module. GetOperator() and GetOperand(), because they are
defined in main.cpp, can use this variable, even though they will be called
from inside the ExternalInterfaceModule. This is an important feature for
callbacks, allowing them to modify the state of their home module or use
its variables or functions, and shows one of the few good uses of global
variables.

Line 21 uses the `bool` function *fstreamvariable*`.is_open()` to check whether or not the `TapeInputStream` has been opened, and line 22 uses the `bool` function *fstreamvariable*`.eof()` to check whether or not it has reached the end of the file. If the input stream has not been opened or has reached the end of the commands in the file, control flows to line 29, where the next operator is instead obtained from `cin`. This means the program will work if you provide no filename, if the file exists but is empty, or if the file has some commands in it. If the input stream is open and has not reached the end of the file, line 21 gets the operator from the `TapeInputStream`.

Lines 39–50 serve the same function for the operand.

The `TapeInputStream` is opened in lines 64–80.

Line 64 checks the number of words on the command line (`argc` stands for "argument count") to see whether there is a file path. If so, line 69 opens the `TapeInputStream` using that path.

Line 99 is performed when the user has entered the . operator to indicate that the program should stop. It closes the `TapeInputStream` so that `Tape()` can open the file for output.

Line 102 tells the `Tape()` to stream itself out and then delete its storage. This line used to be in `CalculateFromInput()`, but it has been moved here instead, so that `argv[1]` doesn't have to be passed into `CalculateFromInput()`.

Summing Up

A relatively small number of changes have made it possible for the calculator to remember where you left off each time, and to return to that state using a tape file as input. You have seen how to define a stream variable, how to open it for output and input, and how to close it. You have seen how to use the inserter to write to the stream and the extractor to read from the stream. You are now ready to move on to creating your first C++ objects.

LESSON 17

Classes: Structures with Functions

In this lesson, you will learn about the basics of classes and the components that make up classes.

The Class as a Mini-Program

In previous lessons, you have seen almost everything you need for an easy understanding of *class* types. You have learned to define and use functions for processing and to define and use structs to contain data. Now you will learn about *classes*, which are structs with member functions as well as member variables, and which can both contain and process data.

A variable of a class type is usually referred to as an *object*.

Just as a program's or function's internal state is based on the content of its variables, an object's internal state is based on the content of its member variables. The content of member variables can change as control flows through the member functions of an object, and the object will retain those changes for the next member function call. Member variables of an object can be simple, structured, enumerated, or class types.

Member functions are just like any other functions, except that they have access to member variables without needing to use the member selection operator.

Classes Versus Instances

A class and an object of a class are not the same thing, any more than blueprints and buildings are the same. A class describes the objects that can be created from it.

You create an object by creating an *instance* of a class—that is, by defining a variable of the type of the class. This is called *instantiation*.

The member variables of an object come into existence when the object is instantiated and are automatically destroyed when the object is destroyed.

Objects can be instantiated on the stack or from the heap, like any other variables. An object is destroyed when the program terminates, when it is deleted, or when its variable goes out of scope.

Declaring a Class

You can see that a class declaration looks just like a struct declaration, except that it uses the keyword class:

```
class classname
{
    members
};
```

Some classes have only member variables, but most have member functions as well.

If you were to make the accumulator into a class, you might create the following:

```
class aSAMSAccumulator
{
    float myAccumulator;
    void Accumulate(char theOperator,float theOperand = 0);
};
```

There's only one problem here. Unlike a struct, in which members are normally public and accessible to your program, class members are normally private (this enforces *information hiding*, also called *encapsulation*, as the basic characteristic of the class). Though you can see these members by reading the declaration, no part of the program can use them. So neither myAccumulator nor the Accumulate() function is available to your program—it is as if they were defined in the implementation part of the module, and not in the header.

To make the `Accumulate()` function available (or *public*), you need to use the `public:` keyword (one of several *visibility* keywords) in the class declaration. Listing 17.1 demonstrates the use of this keyword.

LISTING 17.1 The `public:` Keyword

```
 1: class aSAMSAccumulator
 2: {
 3:     float myAccumulator;
 4:
*5:     public:
 6:
 7:         void Accumulate
               ➥(char theOperator,float theOperand = 0);
 8: };
```

The `public:` keyword is effective until the end of the class declaration or until a different visibility keyword is encountered (for instance, `private:`).

It's usually a good idea to use the `private:` keyword, just to make sure that you don't accidentally turn private members into public members, or public members into private members. Listing 17.2 shows the use of this keyword.

LISTING 17.2 The `private:` Keyword

```
 1: class aSAMSAccumulator
 2: {
*3:     private:
 4:
 5:         float myAccumulator;
 6:
 7:     public:
 8:
 9:         void Accumulate
               ➥(char theOperator,float theOperand = 0);
10: };
```

Header and Implementation

The header file for a class contains the class declaration, which declares member variables and member functions. The implementation file contains the member function definitions.

Because a class effectively functions as a namespace, namespaces are not as commonly used with class header and implementation files. However, #ifndef, #define, and #endif are still always a part of the header file for the usual reasons.

Normally, a module contains the declaration and definition of only one class, but the compiler does not enforce this.

In the implementation file for the module, each member function for the class must be defined. To identify a function as a member of the class, the header for the function has the name of the function prefixed by the name of the class:

```
type classname::functionname(arguments)
{
    body
}
```

The use of the *scope resolution operator* (::), which you previously used with namespaces, tells the compiler the name of the class where the function is declared and allows the compiler to make sure that the declaration matches the definition.

It also allows this function to use the public and private members of the class without the member selection operator.

Calling Class Member Functions

Member functions are called from outside the object using the same member selection (.) and pointer member selection (->) operators you used with structs to access member variables (see Listing 17.3).

LISTING 17.3   The Member Selection and Pointer Member Selection Operators in Use

```
 1: aSAMSAccumulator AccumulatorInstance;
 2:
 3: aSAMSAccumulator *AccumulatorInstancePointer =
 4:     new aSAMSAccumulator;
 5:
*6: AccumulatorInstance.Accumulate('+',34);
*7: AccumulatorInstancePointer->Accumulate('-',34);
```

Types Nested Within Classes

Because the class often takes on the role of the namespace, related types may be declared in the public section of the class. For instance, the anOperator enumerated type can be declared in aSAMSAccumulator class, as shown in Listing 17.4.

LISTING 17.4   An enum Within a Class Declaration

```
 1: class aSAMSAccumulator
 2: {
 3:     private:
 4:
 5:         float myAccumulator;
 6:
 7:     public:
 8:
*9:         enum anOperator
*10:            {add,subtract,multiply,divide,query,reset};
11:
12:         void Accumulate
13:         (
14:             anOperator theOperator,
15:             float theOperand = 0
16:         );
17: };
```

To declare a variable of the nested type outside the class, use the scope resolution operator, just as if the type were in a namespace:

```
aSAMSAccumulator Accumulator;
Accumulator.Accumulate(aSAMSAccumulator::add,34);
```

This applies not only to such nested enumerated types, but also to nested structured and class types.

This use of the scope resolution operator does not apply to instance member functions. They are found as a result of your use of the member selection operator on the object name.

Constructors and Destructors

When you create a struct variable, the value of the member variables is not defined until you initialize them from your program. But the class allows you to declare and define a special member function, the *constructor*, which can initialize member variables, public or private, when an object of the class is instantiated.

The constructor is called automatically by code that the compiler generates as part of the process of instantiating the object.

The constructor has the same name as the class. It has no return type, not even void, and the most basic constructor has no arguments. For a class called aSAMSAccumulator, it would be specified in the class declaration as shown in Listing 17.5.

LISTING 17.5   A Constructor in aSAMSAccumulator

```
 1: class aSAMSAccumulator
 2: {
 3:     private:
 4:
 5:         float myAccumulator;
 6:
 7:     public:
 8:
 9:         enum anOperator
10:             {add,subtract,multiply,divide,query,reset};
11:
*12:         aSAMSAccumulator(void);
13:
14:         void Accumulate
15:         (
16:             anOperator theOperator,
17:             float theOperand = 0
18:         );
19: };
```

The constructor should be declared in the public section of the class declaration, generally after any public types and before any public member functions. A private constructor means the class cannot be instantiated, and though this has an occasional use, it is very rare.

The Constructor Initializer Section

While a normal or member function in an implementation file is defined by a head and a body, a constructor has an additional section between the two, used specifically to define the initialization of member variables. For example, the following code initializes the member variable myAccumulator to zero for each object that is instantiated from the class:

```
aSAMSAccumulator::aSAMSAccumulator(void): myAccumulator(0)
{
}
```

You can also initialize member variables in the constructor function body. Usually this is more appropriate when the initialization is complex enough to require some decisions or functions to be performed as part of the initialization.

An initialization section consists of the names of member variables separated by commas, with each variable name followed by an initial value in parentheses. These are referred to as *initializers*. In this case the initial value is a literal.

The Constructor Body

The prototype for a constructor is declared in the class declaration of the header file for the module, while the body of the constructor is defined in the implementation file, just as with any member function. Don't forget that the constructor has no return type, or you will get a compiler error message.

Constructors with Arguments

The basic or *default constructor* has no arguments, but constructors can have arguments. The declaration of constructor arguments is just like the declaration of member function arguments. For instance:

```
aSAMSAccumulator(float theInitialAccumulatorValue);
```

You usually provide arguments to a constructor so you can control the initialization of a private member variable, as in

```
aSAMSAccumulator::aSAMSAccumulator
    (float theInitialAccumulatorValue):
        myAccumulator(theInitialAccumulatorValue)
{
}
```

You can see here that the initialization for the member variable is no longer a literal. This time it is a formal argument.

The following variant is allowed, but the preceding form of the definition is preferred:

```
aSAMSAccumulator::aSAMSAccumulator
    ➡(float theInitialAccumulatorValue)
{
    myAccumulator = theInitialAccumulatorValue;
}
```

Multiple Constructors

With all these different kinds of constructors, you might wonder how to choose between them. With many programming problems, when confronted with a multiple-choice question, the best answer is to pick all the alternatives, and this is true for constructors.

A class can have several constructors (see Listing 17.6), and the compiler will call the one used where the class is instantiated.

LISTING 17.6   Multiple Constructors in aSAMSAccumulator

```
 1: class aSAMSAccumulator
 2: {
 3:     private:
 4:
 5:         float myAccumulator;
 6:
 7:     public:
 8:
 9:         enum anOperator
10:             {add,subtract,multiply,divide,query,reset};
11:
*12:         aSAMSAccumulator(void);
*13:         aSAMSAccumulator(float theInitialAccumulatorValue);
14:
15:         void Accumulate
16:         (
17:             anOperator theOperator,
18:             float theOperand = 0
19:         );
20: };
```

This allows an instance to be created either by using the default initialization of myAccumulator to 0 or by providing an initial value for the constructor to assign to myAccumulator:

aSAMSAccumulator FirstAccumulatorValueZero;

or

aSAMSAccumulator SecondAccumulatorValueSpecifiedAs(3);

The compiler can tell which constructor should be used based on the number and type of arguments that follow the name of the variable. If there are no arguments, the default constructor is used.

Destructors

Not only will the compiler generate code to call the constructor of your choice when an object is instantiated, it will also be willing to generate code to call another special member function, the *destructor*, when the object either goes out of scope or is deleted.

A destructor has the name of the class and should be prefixed with "virtual ~" or "~" (~ is called a *tilde*). Listing 17.7 shows a destructor.

LISTING 17.7   A Destructor in aSAMSAccumulator

```
 1: class aSAMSAccumulator
 2: {
 3:     private:
 4:
 5:         float myAccumulator;
 6:
 7:     public:
 8:
 9:         enum anOperator
10:             {add,subtract,multiply,divide,query,reset};
11:
12:         aSAMSAccumulator(void);
13:         aSAMSAccumulator(float theInitialAccumulatorValue);
14:
*15:         virtual ~aSAMSAccumulator(void);
16:
17:         void Accumulate
```

LISTING 17.7 Continued

```
18:         (
19:             anOperator theOperator,
20:             float theOperand = 0
21:         );
22: };
```

Line 15 shows the destructor for this class. There are situations in which the virtual keyword is not needed, but it is always safer to provide it, for reasons that will become clear in Lesson 22, "Inheritance."

There can be only one destructor, and it never has either a return type or an argument.

Usually, you only need a destructor when you allocate member variables from the heap. An object should call delete on its heap-allocated member variable storage in the destructor, preventing a memory leak.

The Copy Constructor and When You Need It

There is one special form of constructor with arguments: the copy constructor (see Listing 17.8).

This is used so that you can create an object whose state is exactly the same as the state of another object of the same class.

LISTING 17.8 A Copy Constructor in aSAMSAccumulator

```
1: class aSAMSAccumulator
2: {
3:     private:
4:
5:         float myAccumulator;
6:
7:     public:
8:
9:         enum anOperator
            ➥{add,subtract,multiply,divide,query,reset};
10:
11:         aSAMSAccumulator(void);
```

LISTING 17.8 Continued

```
12:        aSAMSAccumulator(float theInitialAccumulatorValue);
*13:       aSAMSAccumulator
               ➥(aSAMSAccumulator theOtherAccumulator);
14:
15:        virtual ~aSAMSAccumulator(void);
16:
17:        void Accumulate
               ➥(char theOperator,float theOperand = 0);
18: };
```

aSAMSAccumulator has a copy constructor, which might be
implemented as

```
aSAMSAccumulator::aSAMSAccumulator
   (aSAMSAccumulator theOtherAccumulator)::
   myAccumulator(theOtherAccumulator.myAccumulator)
{
}
```

One of the interesting things in this definition is the use of a private member variable of theOtherAccumulator: myAccumulator. This is allowed
because theOtherAccumulator is an instance of the same class as the
object whose copy constructor is called.

A copy constructor will only be used when an object is instantiated, as
follows:

```
aSAMSAccumulator SecondAccumulatorValueSpecifiedAs(3);

aSAMSAccumulator CopyOfSecondAccumulator
   (SecondAccumulatorValueSpecifiedAs);
```

In this case, CopyOfSecondAccumulator will start with a value of 3.

Relaxing "Declare Before Use" Within Classes

Members of a class are declared in the class declaration. In the implementation, the order of declarations in the class does not affect visibility, so a
member function declared first in the class can call on a function declared

fifth. In effect, every member in the class declaration is visible to every member function implementation.

This does not hold true within the class declaration. The following would be invalid because anOperator has not been declared before it is used for a formal argument in Accumulate():

```
void Accumulate
(
    anOperator theOperator,
    float theOperand = 0
);
enum anOperator
    {add,subtract,multiply,divide,query,reset};
```

Summing Up

In this lesson, you have seen that classes are like structs with member functions. You have been introduced to the public and private visibility keywords and have learned that classes have special functions called constructors and destructors to allow for initialization and for freeing heap-allocated storage before destruction. You have seen that a class can have multiple constructors, including a copy constructor. Finally, you have seen how to declare types within a class declaration and use them outside the class.

LESSON 18

Refactoring the Calculator with Classes

In this lesson, you'll analyze the calculator and get ready to turn it into classes.

Moving Functions into Classes

The calculator you've constructed so far is not very different from an object-oriented C++ program. This lesson will document an object-oriented design of the calculator to show the differences.

The UML Diagram

The *Unified Modeling Language (UML)* is a standard way of drawing diagrams of object-oriented programs regardless of language. There are several types of UML diagrams, but you will be looking at only one of these: the *class diagram*.

A class diagram shows the classes that make up a program and their *relationships* (UML also calls these *associations*)—especially whether one class has member variables of another class. There is a single block for each class, and each block is divided into sections for the class name, the member variables (called *attributes* in UML), and the member functions (called *operations* in UML).

Figure 18.1 shows an example of a class.

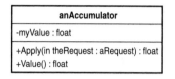

FIGURE **18.1**   A class block from a UML class diagram.

This example shows the class `anAccumulator`. It has a member variable `myValue`, which is a `float`. The minus sign (`-`) before the member variable name indicates that the member variable is private. The type of the member variable is shown after the member variable name, with a colon (`:`) separating the two.

The class also has two member functions: `Apply()`, which takes `aRequest` as a `const` (also called an input or "in") argument and returns a `float`, and `Value()`, which has no arguments and returns a `float`.

Both functions are prefixed with a plus sign (`+`) to indicate that they are public.

Default constructors are not shown, though they could be. The diagram must show any constructor with arguments and any destructor.

A UML Diagram for the Calculator

Figure 18.2 shows what the calculator looks like as a set of classes.

This is a UML class diagram of the entire `SAMSCalculator` namespace, which is the only namespace you will use in the object-oriented version of the calculator.

You can see five classes and a UML *datatype* (any non-class type is a UML datatype). This datatype is the familiar `anOperator` enumerated type. In the discussion that follows, some of what is stated is not visible in the diagram, but can be understood by inference from names and argument types.

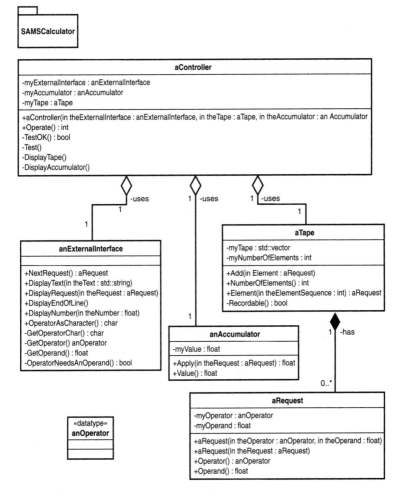

FIGURE 18.2 The calculator as a UML class diagram.

The classes are

- aController, which is given anExternalInterface,
  anAccumulator, and aTape. It keeps references to these internally, but does not own them. Their life spans are not the same

as that of the controller, as is shown by the connection from
aController to the *used* classes. The unfilled diamond on the
connecting lines shows that a *shared* object of the connected
class "plugs in" to a parent object.

Object Life Span   The time between the instantiation
of the object and the destruction of the object. The
object is instantiated either when it is defined as a
variable or when it is allocated from the heap. It is
destroyed either by going out of scope or by being
deleted.

- anExternalInterface, which controls all the input and output
  for the calculator. The controller uses this for all input and output. anExternalInterface lets the controller use GetRequest(),
  which returns aRequest, and it can also display aRequest, text,
  or a number.

- anAccumulator, which aController uses to apply aRequest's
  Operand() to anAccumulator. Apply() does so based on
  aRequest's Operator(). Both Apply() and Value() return the
  current myValue for anAccumulator.

- aTape, which aController uses to record aRequest. aTape contains myTape, an std::vector of aRequest to which aTape's
  Add() function adds the operator and operand of each operation.
  Like iostream, std::vector is a part of the Standard C++
  library, and is much the same thing you had in the previous version of the program, where you made the tape from a linked list
  of aTapeElement.

  aTape can provide its NumberOfElements() and any specific
  Element() as requested. aTape can have any number of
  aRequest objects whose life spans it controls; this is shown by
  the solid diamond on the connector from aTape to aRequest and
  by the 0..* at the aRequest end.

- aRequest, which has private member variables myOperator and myOperand. aRequest is passed to every class in the program and returned by member functions in two of them. It has a constructor that accepts theOperator and theOperand, and a copy constructor, which is used when aRequest is added to aTape. This makes it possible for aTape to have its own copy of aRequest, which it can then get rid of when it needs to.

  Member functions Operator() and Operand() provide the values of aRequest's private member variables to other classes. Note that there is no way to change these variables once an object has been instantiated from the class, because the variables are private and the functions are only provided to get their values, not to set them.

This diagram can be your guide when you reconstruct the calculator as an object-oriented program.

Differences

PromptModule and ErrorHandlingModule no longer exist. Their functions will be placed in anExternalInterface and in aController.

Some names have been changed to make the classes more readable. These include the Accumulate() function, which is now Apply (so you can code Accumulator.Apply()), and the internal value anAccumulator, now called myValue, which can be obtained through the Value() function.

In the next lesson, you will make more comprehensive use of what used to be aTapeElement. Accordingly, it has been given a more general name—aRequest. In fact, this is now the core object of the calculator.

Summing Up

You have looked at the Unified Modeling Language, a standard form of documentation for object-oriented programs in any language. You have learned to read the basics of a UML class diagram and have seen how the diagram indicates classes, methods, arguments, return types, public/ private status, and which classes use or have instances of other classes as members. You have reviewed the differences between the old and the new program as represented by this diagram. This diagram of the calculator will be helpful when you turn it into an object-oriented program.

LESSON 19

Implementing the Calculator as Classes

In this lesson, you will review your knowledge of classes while looking at some classes from the reimplemented calculator.

Class Notation

As you saw earlier, there are two parts to a class: the class declaration, which goes in the module header file, and the class definition, which goes in the module implementation file.

The class declaration for a simple class, such as aRequest, shows most of the notation used for a class definition (see Listing 19.1).

LISTING 19.1 aRequest **Header**

```
 *1: #ifndef RequestModuleH
 *2: #define RequestModuleH
  3:
 *4: namespace SAMSCalculator
 *5: {
 *6:     class aRequest
 *7:     {
  8:         public:
  9:
*10:             enum anOperator
*11:             {
*12:                 add,
*13:                 subtract,
*14:                 multiply,
*15:                 divide,
*16:                 query,
```

LISTING 19.1   Continued

```
 *17:               reset,
 *18:               selftest,
 *19:               querytape,
 *20:               stop
 *21:           };
  22:
  23:           // Note: There is no default constructor
  24:           // you must provide an operator and operand when
  25:           // creating an instance of this class
  26:
 *27:           aRequest
 *28:           (
 *29:               const anOperator theOperator,
 *30:               const float anOperand
 *31:           );
  32:
  33:           // Allow a copy
  34:
 *35:           aRequest(const aRequest &theRequest);
  36:
  37:           // You cannot change the operator or operand
  38:           // after an instance of this class is created;
  39:           // you can only get their values
  40:
 *41:           anOperator Operator(void) const;
 *42:           float Operand(void) const;
  43:
 *44:       private:
  45:
 *46:           anOperator myOperator;
 *47:           float myOperand;
 *48:     };
 *49: };
  50:
 *51: #endif
```

ANALYSIS   Lines 1, 2, and 51 are familiar from the old version's header files. They prevent a compiler message such as

```
[C++ Error] RequestModule.h(11):
E2238 Multiple declaration for 'aRequest'
```

Lines 4, 5, and 49 bracket the class declaration in a namespace, so that if some other library declares a class called aRequest, there will be no *name clash*.

Lines 6, 7, and 48 make up the block that declares the class, which is identified by the keyword class.

Lines 10–21 declare the enumerated type anOperator as part of this class.

Lines 27–31 and 35 are the primary constructor and the copy constructor. A default constructor is not declared. Because of this, any attempt to define aRequest Request would cause the following compiler error message:

```
[C++ Error] ControllerModule.cpp(20):
E2285 Could not find a match for 'aRequest::aRequest()'
```

The lack of a default constructor ensures that anyone using aRequest will be forced to initialize it correctly with theOperator and theOperand.

Lines 46 and 47 are the definitions for myOperator and myOperand.

Lines 41 and 42 are the *getter* functions for myOperator and myOperand. They return the current value of those members and are marked as const. This means that they will not change any member variables in the class.

The Private and Public Members of aRequest

You can see that the declaration of myOperator and myOperand is in the private section of the class declaration (line 44 starts that section). Because they are in the private section, these variables cannot be changed by anything except member functions of the class.

Because the constructor sets these variables, and the only member functions that deal with them do nothing but return their values, they cannot be changed once the object is instantiated.

Member variables should usually be private. The class can then selectively expose the current content (provide getter functions only), allow the current content to be changed but not reveal the current value (provide setter functions only), or allow both (provide both getter and setter functions).

Initialization

Listing 19.2 shows the definition (implementation) of the class aRequest.

LISTING 19.2   aRequest Implementation

```
 *1: #include "RequestModule.h"
  2:
 *3: namespace SAMSCalculator
 *4: {
 *5:     aRequest::aRequest
            ➡(
                ➡const anOperator theOperator,
                ➡const float theOperand
            ➡):
 *6:         myOperator(theOperator),
 *7:         myOperand(theOperand)
 *8:     {
 *9:     };
 10:
*11:     aRequest::aRequest(const aRequest &theRequest):
*12:         myOperator(theRequest.myOperator),
*13:         myOperand(theRequest.myOperand)
*14:     {
*15:     }
 16:
 17:     aRequest::anOperator aRequest::Operator(void) const
 18:     {
 19:         return myOperator;
 20:     };
 21:
 22:     float aRequest::Operand(void) const
 23:     {
 24:         return myOperand;
 25:     };
*26: };
```

ANALYSIS Line 1 includes the class declaration header file so that the compiler can check this definition against the declaration and make sure they are consistent with each other.

Lines 3 and 26 wrap the functions in the namespace that holds the class declaration, allowing the compiler to check them against that declaration.

Line 5 defines the primary constructor with its two arguments. This is one of two ways that an instance of this class can be initialized (the other is the copy constructor on lines 11–15. Lines 6 and 7 perform the initialization of the private member variables myOperator and myOperand from theOperator and theOperand.

You must specify the classname followed by the scope resolution operator before every member function name, or the function implementation cannot be connected to the corresponding member function in the class declaration.

Don't Forget *classname*:: on Every Member Function
This is a common error, and the compiler does not catch it until you link the program, at which point you will usually get a message such as

```
[Linker Error] Unresolved external
'SAMSCalculator::aController::TestOK
(SAMSCalculator::anAccumulator&,
const SAMSCalculator::aRequest&, const float) const'
from ObjectOrientedCalculator.cpp
```

Lines 11–15 define the copy constructor, whose sole argument is a reference to another instance of this same class. The initializers in lines 12 and 13 set myOperator and myOperand from theRequest.myOperator and theRequest.myOperand. Remember that only a copy constructor can access member variables in the private section of another instance, and that it should not be used as a way to modify the other instance of the class.

Lines 17 and 22 mark the getter functions as const (they will not modify member variables) at the end of each function head.

Internal State

The internal state of aRequest is represented by myOperator and
myOperand. The functions on lines 17–35 of the implementation allow
other classes or code to get those values.

If you refer back to Figure 18.2 in Lesson 18, "Refactoring the Calculator
with Classes," you will see that not all classes have internal state. For
instance, anExternalInterface has no member variables at all.

Instances of classes such as aRequest have a single internal state for their
entire life span, because their member variables cannot be changed.

Instances of classes such as anAccumulator have an internal state that
changes frequently. Every call to Apply() changes the internal state of
anAccumulator.

Instances of classes such as aController have an indirect internal state.
Their member variables are not changed, but those member variables are
objects that have internal state, and that state can change over time.

Internal state is what makes declaring a function as const so important. If
a function is declared as const, the compiler can verify that it does not
modify class member variables. It can even produce an error message if a
function given a const instance of a class as an argument calls any non-
const member function of that object. So const enables you to be more
certain that every object is being used as intended. You should use const
as often as possible for both arguments and functions to reduce the risk of
any object being misused.

Listing 19.3 shows the implementation of anAccumulator, a class with a
more changeable internal state than aRequest.

LISTING 19.3   anAccumulator Implementation

```
1: #include <string>
2: #include <exception>
3: #include <io stream>
4: #include "AccumulatorModule.h"
5:
6: namespace SAMSCalculator
7: {
```

LISTING 19.3   Continued

```
 8:     using namespace std;
 9:
*10:     anAccumulator::anAccumulator(void): myValue(0)
11:     {
12:     };
13:
*14:     anAccumulator::anAccumulator
*15:         (anAccumulator &theAccumulator):
*16:             myValue(theAccumulator.myValue)
17:     {
18:     };
19:
20:     float anAccumulator::Apply(const aRequest &theRequest)
21:     {
22:         switch (theRequest.Operator())
23:         {
*24:             case aRequest::add:
*25:                 myValue+= theRequest.Operand();
*26:                 break;
*27:
*28:             case aRequest::subtract:
*29:                 myValue-= theRequest.Operand();
*30:                 break;
*31:
*32:             case aRequest::multiply:
*33:                 myValue*= theRequest.Operand();
*34:                 break;
*35:
*36:             case aRequest::divide:
*37:                 myValue/= theRequest.Operand();
*38:                 break;
39:
*40:             default:
*41:
*42:                 throw
*43:                     runtime_error
*44:                     (
*45:                         string("SAMSCalculator::") +
*46:                         string("anAccumulator::") +
*47:                         string("Apply") +
*48:                         string(" - Unknown operator.")
*49:                     );
50:         };
51:
```

LISTING 19.3 Continued

```
52:          return Value();
53:     };
54:
55:     float anAccumulator::Value(void) const
56:     {
57:          return myValue;
58:     };
59: };
```

ANALYSIS Line 10 of the implementation initializes myValue to 0 for the case in which anAccumulator is instantiated with the default constructor.

Lines 14–16 are the head and initialization for the copy constructor. myValue for the current instance is set to the content of myValue from the argument theAccumulator.

When either constructor finishes, the object has been created, and the member variable, myValue, is in a safe and usable state. If you do not initialize a member variable, it might contain any random value. This is why constructors are so important.

It is also the reason you do not see public member variables in well-written classes. Assignment to public member variables cannot be controlled, and nothing prevents assignment of an inappropriate value at an inappropriate time. But member function code can inspect and validate an incoming value, so use of getters and setters is more certain to keep the object's internal state consistent across the object's lifetime.

Lines 24–38 change the state of the member variable myValue when a call to Apply() is made on an instance of anAccumulator. The code uses the shorthand arithmetic assignment operators +=, -=, *=, and /= to make these changes.

Lines 40–49 deal with the possibility of receiving an unanticipated operator by throwing a runtime_error exception. You will notice that the exception reports the namespace, class, and function where the error is detected as well as the message. This can help when debugging.

You will also notice the use of the Standard C++ library `string` class (from the `#include` `<string>` header, `std` namespace) to produce the message in this exception throw. The `std::string` class allows you to join several strings into one with +, much as using several << operators with `cout` will display multiple variables on a single line of output. `string()` is the constructor for the `string` class, and converts the C++ string literal (really a `char *`) to a `std::string`.

Naming

Despite the move to classes and object-orientation, not much has changed about how things are named. As before, types are prefixed with "a" or "an," while formal arguments are prefixed with "the." You can see how this makes it easy to understand the scope, source, and life span of variables and their content, and to distinguish a class declaration from an instance of the class.

In addition, use of the prefix "my" is continued, but in a slightly different context.

In the procedural `Accumulator()` function, `myAccumulator` was a static local variable whose life span was the same as the program. It provided `Accumulator()` with internal state and made it more like an object. In the case of classes, the prefix "my" is used for member variables, and indicates essentially the same thing: "This variable is part of the internal state of the object—it is `mywhatever`."

The only difference is that now the life span of that variable is the same as the life span of the object, rather than the life span of the program.

In addition, every call to `Accumulator()` affected the same `myAccumulator` variable. That is still true in the sense that every caller to `Apply()` on the same instance of `anAccumulator` affects the same `myValue`; however, as you will see in the `SelfTest()` function, it is now possible to have more than one instance of `anAccumulator`, each with its own separate `myValue`.

Some programmers follow other naming standards. Some make the variable type part of the name, others use first letter capitalization to distinguish between class and instance. The naming convention used in this book, however, focuses on what can be the most important issues for object-oriented programmers—object ownership, source of variable content, object life span, and the distinction between class, instance, and formal argument.

Moving Function Content into Member Functions

In the implementation of anAccumulator, you moved the content of the Accumulator() function into the Apply() function with minimal changes. Next, take a look at the header and implementation files for aController, which embodies much of what used to be in the Calculator() function (see Listings 19.4 and 19.5).

LISTING 19.4   aController Header

```
 1: #ifndef ControllerModuleH
 2: #define ControllerModuleH
 3:
 4: #include "ExternalInterfaceModule.h"
 5: #include "AccumulatorModule.h"
 6: #include "TapeModule.h"
 7:
 8: namespace SAMSCalculator
 9: {
10:    class aController
11:    {
12:       public:
13:
14:          aController
15:          (
16:             anExternalInterface &theExternalInterface,
17:             anAccumulator &theAccumulator,
18:             aTape &theTape
19:          );
20:
21:          int Operate(void);
22:
23:       private:
24:
*25:          anExternalInterface &myExternalInterface;
```

LISTING 19.4   Continued

```
*26:            anAccumulator &myAccumulator;
*27:            aTape &myTape;
 28:
 29:            bool TestOK
 30:            (
 31:                anAccumulator &theAccumulator,
 32:                const aRequest &theRequest,
 33:                const float theExpectedResult
 34:
 35:            ) const;
 36:
 37:            void SelfTest(void) const;
 38:            void DisplayAccumulator(void) const;
 39:            void DisplayTape(void) const;
 40:        };
 41: };
 42:
 43: #endif
```

The header is straightforward, so let's begin an examination of the implementation with a look at the constructor in Listing 19.5.

LISTING 19.5   aController Constructor

```
 1:        aController::aController
 2:        (
 3:            anExternalInterface &theExternalInterface,
 4:            anAccumulator &theAccumulator,
 5:            aTape &theTape
 6:        ):
 7:            myExternalInterface(theExternalInterface),
 8:            myAccumulator(theAccumulator),
 9:            myTape(theTape)
10:        {
11:        };
```

ANALYSIS There is no default constructor, so this is the constructor that must be used to make aController. It requires
theExternalInterface, theAccumulator, and theTape as arguments. The arguments are references to instances of the indicated classes. In lines 25–27 of the aController header, you can see the member variables that are initialized are also references.

Normally, you may recall, the compiler will not allow you to assign anything to a reference once the reference has been defined. However, the references in lines 25–27 of the declaration have only been *declared* at that point. As far as the compiler is concerned, they are not defined until the flow of control has reached the constructor body. Therefore, these references can be initialized by the constructor initializer section in lines 16–18 of the implementation.

Next, let's look at a change to the SelfTest() function in Listing 19.6.

LISTING 19.6   aController SelfTest() Function

```
 1:      void aController::SelfTest(void) const
 2:      {
*3:          anAccumulator TestAccumulator;
 4:
 5:          try
 6:          {
 7:              if
 8:                  (
*9:                      TestOK
*10:                     (
*11:                         TestAccumulator,
*12:                         aRequest(aRequest::add,3),
*13:                         3
*14:                     )
 15:                     &&
 16:                     TestOK
 17:                     (
 18:                         TestAccumulator,
 19:                         aRequest(aRequest::subtract,2),
 20:                         1
 21:                     )
 22:                     &&
 23:                     TestOK
 24:                     (
 25:                         TestAccumulator,
 26:                         aRequest(aRequest::multiply,4),
 27:                         4
 28:                     )
 29:                     &&
 30:                     TestOK
 31:                     (
 32:                         TestAccumulator,
```

LISTING 19.6   Continued

```
33:                           aRequest(aRequest::divide,2),
34:                    2
35:                 )
36:              )
37:           {
38:              cout << "Test OK." << endl;
39:           }
40:           else
41:           {
42:              cout << "Test failed." << endl;
43:           };
44:        }
45:        catch (...)
46:        {
47:           cout << "Test failed because of an exception.";
48:        };
49:     };
```

ANALYSIS   Line 3 shows one of the most important differences from the procedural version: This `SelfTest()` function instantiates anAccumulator and performs all tests on that object, rather than on `myAccumulator`. This avoids disruption of the current calculator internal state and simplifies testing. The `TestOK()` function has been modified to use this object, which is provided as an argument. Lines 9–14 show such a call.

The `SelfTest()` `TestAccumulator` will be destroyed when `SelfTest()` is done. This will have no effect on `aController`'s `myAccumulator`.

Line 12 shows the `aRequest` constructor being used in the actual arguments to `TestOK()` to create a temporary request for use by the test.

Next, let's look at the use of one of the references provided by `main()` to the constructor of `aController` (see Listing 19.7).

LISTING 19.7   `aController DisplayTape()` Function

```
1:     void aController::DisplayTape(void) const
2:     {
3:        int NumberOfElements = myTape.NumberOfElements();
4:
```

LISTING 19.7   Continued

```
  5:        for
           ➥(
               ➥int Index = 0;
               ➥Index < NumberOfElements;
               ➥Index++
           ➥)
  6:        {
  7:            myExternalInterface.
                   ➥DisplayRequest(myTape.Element(Index));
  8:            myExternalInterface.DisplayEndOfLine();
  9:        };
 10:
 11:        DisplayAccumulator();
 12:    };
```

ANALYSIS   In line 7, myExternalInterface function DisplayRequest() is used to take care of displaying the request Operator() and Operand().

Finally, the Operate() function implements the real control flow of the calculator, as shown in Listing 19.8.

LISTING 19.8   aController Operate() Function

```
  1:    int aController::Operate(void)
  2:    {
 *3:        aRequest Request =
               ➥myExternalInterface.NextRequest();
  4:
 *5:        while (Request.Operator() != aRequest::stop)
  6:        {
  7:            try
  8:            {
 *9:                switch (Request.Operator())
 10:                {
*11:                case aRequest::selftest:
 12:
 13:                    SelfTest();
 14:                    break;
 15:
*16:                case aRequest::querytape:
 17:
 18:                    DisplayTape();
 19:                    break;
```

LISTING 19.8   Continued

```
 20:
*21:                    case aRequest::query:
 22:
 23:                        DisplayAccumulator();
 24:                        break;
 25:
 26:                    default:
 27:
*28:                        myTape.Add(Request);
*29:                        myAccumulator.Apply(Request);
 30:
 31:                };
 32:
 33:                Request = myExternalInterface.NextRequest();
 34:            }
*35:            catch (runtime_error RuntimeError)
 36:            {
 37:                cerr << "Runtime error: " <<
                        ➥RuntimeError.what() << endl;
 38:            }
*39:            catch (...)
 40:            {
 41:                cerr <<
 42:                    "Non runtime_error exception " <<
                        ➥"caught in Controller.Operate." <<
 43:                    endl;
 44:            };
 45:        };
 46:
 47:        return 0;
 48:    };
```

ANALYSIS   Line 3 gets aRequest from myExternalInterface and line 5 loops as long as the Operator() is not aRequest::stop.

Line 9 shows that the switch statement can use the enum nested within the aRequest class.

Lines 11, 16, and 21 are cases receiving the flow of control based on the Request.Operator() tested in line 9.

Lines 28 and 29 use myTape and myAccumulator to perform the central functions of the calculator.

And, of course, lines 35 and 39 catch any exceptions without allowing the loop to be interrupted.

The Object as Callback Structure

In Lesson 15, "Structures and Types," you passed a struct with function pointers into Calculator() to get it to perform a *callback* on the correct input and output functions from main.cpp. aController gets a set of objects from the outside and coordinates them to perform correct actions by calling their member functions. These similar patterns show another link between concepts of procedural programming and concepts of object-oriented programming.

Who Allocates, Who Deletes, Who Uses, What's Shared

The ownership of objects is one of the most important concerns in object-oriented programming. In the case of theAccumulator, theExternalInterface, and theTape passed to aController, the instances are owned by the part of the program that defined the instance of aController (in this case, main()). aController is not empowered to get rid of these objects, because it only has references to them. However, the compiler does not enforce this policy, so you must.

Other classes, such as aRequest and anAccumulator, retain complete ownership over their member variable storage, which is created and destroyed along with the instance.

Summing Up

You have looked at several of the new classes that are part of the new calculator and have seen how they are declared and defined. You have seen that their implementations are similar to but slightly different from their procedural counterparts. You have also seen variations in the degree of internal state among classes and differences in the way objects manage storage. And you have seen how to provide an object to another object and then call on it to provide specific services.

LESSON 20

The Rest of the Calculator as Classes

In this lesson you will look at the remainder of the calculator implementation.

Using a Standard C++ Library Class

One of the major changes that object-orientation has made in the work of the programmer is a change in attitude. Where programmers once created everything from scratch, object-oriented programmers first look for classes someone else may have created to do the job.

Obviously, this can be a tremendous benefit to programmer productivity. Whether you are a professional or an amateur, class libraries not only save time, but make it possible to create programs far more powerful than would otherwise be possible. Having a good class library is like having a staff of world-class programmers working for you.

The Standard C++ class library is a good place to start when you need a class to serve a particular purpose and want to know whether it has been written already. Almost every compiler includes this as a standard option.

You can find other class libraries as freeware and shareware on the Internet. The DMOZ Open Directory Project lists PC and Macintosh libraries at `http://dmoz.org/Netscape/Computing_and_Internet/ Shareware/PC/Development_Tools/Components_%26_Libraries/` and `http://dmoz.org/Netscape/Computing_and_Internet/Shareware/MAC/ Development_Tools/Components_%26_Libraries/`, respectively.

It is important to keep in mind that every library creator has different ideas about good names, about the best organization and interface to classes, and about how a library should behave. This means that you will sometimes feel as if you are putting together a machine from wildly varying parts scrounged out of a junkyard. But this is simply an expected cost, regardless of your object-oriented language, and the productivity benefits are so high as to outweigh the minor variations in aesthetics and quality that come from adopting class libraries.

Using a Class Library in aTape

The class aTape is much smaller than the procedural function Tape(). This is partly because the code to save the tape to a file has been removed. (It will be added back again in Lesson 22, "Inheritance.") The other factor contributing to the size decrease is that you will now use the Standard C++ library class vector to hold a list of aRequest objects rather than making your own linked list of aTapeElement structs.

vector is part of the ISO/ANSI Standard C++ class library, so it is safe to adopt it—though it looks very different from the code you have seen so far. It is well tested and has internally consistent naming standards.

Listings 20.1 and 20.2 show the header and implementation of aTape.

LISTING 20.1   aTape Header

```
  1: #ifndef TapeModuleH
  2: #define TapeModuleH
  3:
 *4: #include <vector>
  5:
  6: #include "RequestModule.h"
  7:
  8: namespace SAMSCalculator
  9: {
 10:     class aTape
 11:     {
 12:         public:
 13:
*14:             aTape(void);
 15:
 16:             void Add(const aRequest &theRequest);
 17:             int NumberOfElements(void) const;
```

LISTING 20.1 Continued

```
18:
*19:            aRequest Element
20:                (const int theElementIndex) const;
21:
22:        private:
23:
*24:            std::vector<aRequest> myTape;
25:
26:            bool Recordable
27:                (const aRequest &theRequest) const;
28:    };
29: };
```

 ANALYSIS Line 4 of the class declaration includes <vector> so that line 23 can instantiate an std namespace vector object.

Line 14 declares the default constructor. The compiler, which generates code for a default constructor if one is not defined, does not require this, but it is good practice to always declare the constructor you expect to be used.

Line 24 uses a special declaration to require the vector to only contain aRequest objects. Angle brackets (<>) surround that type.

A copy constructor is not declared for this class.

Compiler-Generated Copy Constructors Can Be Dangerous If a copy constructor is not part of your class and an object of that class is copied, a member-by-member copy will be performed. Such a copy can be dangerous if any members are heap-allocated pointers. A member-by-member copy will copy the pointers, not the storage at the pointer destination. Thus, a copied instance will point to the same member storage as the original, and if one instance changes what is in that storage, both objects will be working with the changed content. This may be what you want, but more commonly it is an error that can be very difficult to track down.

In your case, this is not a problem, because vector will correctly copy its contents in a member-by-member default copy.

LISTING 20.2   aTape Implementation

```
 1: #include <exception>
 2:
 3: #include "TapeModule.h"
 4:
 5: namespace SAMSCalculator
 6: {
 7:     using namespace std;
 8:
*9:     aTape::aTape(void)
*10:    {
*11:    };
 12:
*13:    bool aTape::Recordable
           ➥(const aRequest &theRequest) const
*14:    {
*15:        return // true when
*16:        (
*17:            (theRequest.Operator() == aRequest::add) ||
*18:            (theRequest.Operator() == aRequest::subtract) ||
*19:            (theRequest.Operator() == aRequest::multiply) ||
*20:            (theRequest.Operator() == aRequest::divide) ||
*21:            (theRequest.Operator() == aRequest::reset)
*22:        );
*23:    };
 24:
 25:    void aTape::Add(const aRequest &theRequest)
 26:    {
*27:        if (Recordable(theRequest))
*28:        {
*29:            myTape.push_back(theRequest);
                   ➥// Make a copy of the request, add to end
*30:        };
 31:    };
 32:
 33:    int aTape::NumberOfElements(void) const
 34:    {
*35:        return myTape.size();
 36:    };
 37:
```

LISTING 20.2   Continued

```
 *38:       aRequest aTape::Element
              ⮕(const int theElementIndex) const
  39:       {
 *40:           if (theElementIndex < 0)
  41:           {
  42:               throw
  43:                   runtime_error
  44:                   (
  45:                       string("SAMSCalculator::aTape::") +
  46:                       string("Element") +
  47:                       string(" - Requested element before 0th.")
  48:                   );
  49:           }
  50:
 *51:           if (theElementIndex >= NumberOfElements())
  52:           {
  53:               throw
  54:                   runtime_error
  55:                   (
  56:                       string("SAMSCalculator::aTape::") +
  57:                       string("OperatorAsCharacter") +
  58:                       string(" - Request for element past end.")
  59:                   );
  60:           };
  61:
 *62:           return myTape[theElementIndex];
  63:       };
  64: };
```

ANALYSIS Lines 7–9 of the implementation contain the empty default constructor definition. Even though it does nothing, since you declared it, you must define it.

Lines 27–30 add an element to myTape if Recordable() is true. Recordable(), defined on lines 13–23, is needed because there are requests that should not go on the tape, including aRequest::querytape and aRequest::query. What myTape.Add() stores is aRequest, which means that the character representation of aRequest::anOperator is not present in aTape. This differs from the old Tape() function, which saved the operator character in aTapeElement.

Line 29 adds the request to the myTape vector. You can see that the member function name follows an unusual convention that is common in the Standard C++ class library: It separates words with underscores and uses all lowercase letters.

push_back() creates a copy of theRequest and adds it to the end of the vector. This means that aTape's internal state is safe when the object represented by theRequest reference goes out of scope and is destroyed. If this list were storing references or pointers, the references or pointers might at any time be working with storage that had been *deallocated*, or returned to the heap.

Line 38 defines the getter for an Element(). Lines 40 and 51 ensure that the caller cannot request an element whose sequence is less than zero or greater than the number of elements in the vector. Although vector would probably throw an exception in that situation, you can check these error conditions first and throw what may be a more informative exception. This is one example of the services that can be provided by a getter or setter function. If you just exposed myTape as a public member variable, you would be forced to accept a higher level of risk.

The User Interface in an Object

anExternalInterface takes care of everything in the user interface. However, for this version of the implementation, the code for restoring the calculator state from a saved tape has been removed. As mentioned in the previous lesson, this code will be reintroduced in Lesson 22.

anExternalInterface now contains everything involving communication with the outside world. None of the other classes (except aController, which always sends the SelfTest() results to cout or cerr) communicates with the outside world. Listing 20.3 shows anExternalInterface's header file.

LISTING 20.3   anExternalInterface Header

```
1: #ifndef ExternalInterfaceModuleH
2: #define ExternalInterfaceModuleH
3:
4: #include "RequestModule.h"
```

LISTING 20.3   Continued

```
 5:
 6: namespace SAMSCalculator
 7: {
 8:     class anExternalInterface
 9:     {
10:       public:
11:
12:            anExternalInterface(void);
13:
14:            aRequest NextRequest(void) const;
15:
16:            void DisplayText(const char *theText) const;
17:            void DisplayRequest
                   ➥(const aRequest &theRequest) const;
18:            void DisplayNumber(const float theNumber) const;
19:            void DisplayEndOfLine(void) const;
20:
21:            char OperatorAsCharacter
                   ➥(aRequest::anOperator theOperator) const;
22:
23:       private:
24:
25:            char GetOperatorChar(void) const;
26:            aRequest::anOperator GetOperator(void) const;
27:
28:            bool OperatorNeedsAnOperand
                   ➥(aRequest::anOperator theOperator) const;
29:
30:            float GetOperand(void) const;
31:     };
32: };
33:
34: #endif
```

ANALYSIS   Note the absence of any internal state. There are no member variables in this class.

Line 21 offers a special function that turns aRequest::anOperator back into its string equivalent. This is used for some messages in aController::TestOK() and within this class as well.

Have a look at the implementation. You should start with the constructor (see Listing 20.4), which now has responsibility for setting the cin.exceptions on line 3.

LISTING 20.4   anExternalInterface Constructor

```
1:      anExternalInterface::anExternalInterface(void)
2:      {
*3:         cin.exceptions(cin.failbit);
4:      };
```

Next, Listing 20.5 gets the operator and returns it as
aRequest::anOperator.

LISTING 20.5   anExternalInterface Getting anOperator

```
*1:      char anExternalInterface::GetOperatorChar(void) const
*2:      {
*3:         char OperatorChar;
*4:         cin >> OperatorChar;
*5:         return OperatorChar;
*6:      };
 7:
 8:      aRequest::anOperator anExternalInterface::GetOperator
 9:         (void) const
10:      {
*11:        char OperatorChar = GetOperatorChar();
12:
*13:        switch (OperatorChar)
14:        {
*15:           case '+': return aRequest::add;
*16:           case '-': return aRequest::subtract;
*17:           case '*': return aRequest::multiply;
*18:           case '/': return aRequest::divide;
*19:           case '=': return aRequest::query;
*20:           case '@': return aRequest::reset;
*21:           case '?': return aRequest::querytape;
*22:           case '!': return aRequest::selftest;
*23:           case '.': return aRequest::stop;
24:
*25:           default:
26:
*27:              char OperatorCharAsString[2];
*28:              OperatorCharAsString[0] = OperatorChar;
*29:              OperatorCharAsString[1] = '\0';
30:
*31:              throw
32:                 runtime_error
33:                 (
34:                    string("SAMSCalculator::") +
```

LISTING 20.5   Continued

```
35:                          string("anExternalInterface::") +
36:                          string("GetOperator") +
37:                          string(" - Unknown operator: ") +
38:                          string(OperatorCharAsString)
39:                      );
40:          };
41:      };
```

ANALYSIS Lines 1–6 are the usual code to obtain the operator character. This function is called by line 11, and its result is used in line 13 to control the translation of the character to the aRequest::anOperator in lines 16–23.

Line 25 is the default case for an invalid operator, and lines 27–29 turn the invalid operator character into a string for use in the exception thrown on line 31.

The process of getting the operand, shown in Listing 20.6, is much the same as it was in the procedural version of the program.

LISTING 20.6   anExternalInterface Getting an Operand

```
 *1:     float anExternalInterface::GetOperand(void) const
 *2:     {
 *3:         float Operand;
 *4:
 *5:         try
 *6:         {
 *7:             cin >> Operand;
 *8:         }
 *9:         catch (...)
*10:         {
*11:             // Clear the input stream state
*12:             cin.clear();
*13:
*14:             // Get rid of the pending bad characters
*15:             char BadOperand[5];
*16:             cin >> BadOperand;
*17:
*18:             throw
*19:                 runtime_error
*20:                 (
*21:                     string("SAMSCalculator::") +
*22:                     string("anExternalInterface::") +
```

LISTING 20.6   Continued

```
*23:                    string("GetOperand") +
*24:                    string(" - Not a number: ") +
*25:                    string(BadOperand)
*26:              );
*27:         };
*28:
*29:         return Operand;
*30:    };
```

ANALYSIS   Lines 1–30 get the operand and deal with any error input by throwing an exception that includes the bad characters.

As shown in Listing 20.7, NextRequest() obtains the input and packages it into aRequest.

LISTING 20.7   anExternalInterface Getting a Request

```
 1:    bool anExternalInterface::OperatorNeedsAnOperand
 2:         (aRequest::anOperator theOperator) const
 3:    {
 4:        return
 5:        (
 6:            (theOperator == aRequest::add) ||
 7:            (theOperator == aRequest::subtract) ||
 8:            (theOperator == aRequest::multiply) ||
 9:            (theOperator == aRequest::divide) ||
10:            (theOperator == aRequest::reset)
11:        );
12:    };
13:
14:    aRequest anExternalInterface::NextRequest(void) const
15:    {
16:        aRequest::anOperator Operator = GetOperator();
17:
18:        if (OperatorNeedsAnOperand(Operator))
19:        {
20:            return aRequest(Operator,GetOperand());
21:        }
22:        else
23:        {
24:            return aRequest(Operator,0);
25:        };
26:    };
```

ANALYSIS   Lines 1–12 identify whether a specific operator needs an operand.

Lines 14–26 control getting the operator and operand and packaging them into an aRequest object.

The other functions are largely unchanged except for new functions to convert the operator from enumerated type to character and to display aRequest. These are shown in Listing 20.8.

LISTING 20.8   anExternalInterface Displaying a Request

```
 *1:    char anExternalInterface::OperatorAsCharacter
 *2:        (aRequest::anOperator theOperator) const
 *3:    {
 *4:        switch (theOperator)
 *5:        {
 *6:            case aRequest::add:        return '+';
 *7:            case aRequest::subtract:   return '-';
 *8:            case aRequest::multiply:   return '*';
 *9:            case aRequest::divide:     return '/';
*10:            case aRequest::query:      return '=';
*11:            case aRequest::reset:      return '@';
*12:            case aRequest::querytape:  return '?';
*13:            case aRequest::selftest:   return '!';
*14:
*15:            default:
*16:
*17:                throw
*18:                    runtime_error
*19:                    (
*20:                        string("SAMSCalculator::
                            ➥anExternalInterface::") +
*21:                        string("OperatorAsCharacter
                            ➥" - Unknown operator
                            ➥to be translated.")
*22:                    );
*23:        };
*24:    };
 25:
 26:    void anExternalInterface::DisplayRequest
        ➥(const aRequest &theRequest) const
 27:    {
 28:        cout <<
```

LISTING 20.8   Continued

```
*29:            OperatorAsCharacter(theRequest.Operator()) <<
 30:            theRequest.Operand();
 31:    };
```

 ANALYSIS   Lines 26–31 are used to display the request. Line 29 calls on the OperatorAsCharacter() function to get the operator character for the request. Now, only anExternalInterface knows how to convert characters to and from aRequest::anOperator.

The main.cpp

main.cpp (see Listing 20.9) instantiates everything, hands the objects over to aController, and then starts the Calculator operating.

LISTING 20.9   main.cpp

```
 1: #include "ExternalInterfaceModule.h"
 2: #include "AccumulatorModule.h"
 3: #include "TapeModule.h"
 4: #include "ControllerModule.h"
 5:
 6: int main(int argc, char* argv[])
 7: {
 8:     SAMSCalculator::anExternalInterface
           ➥ExternalInterface;
 9:     SAMSCalculator::anAccumulator            Accumulator;
10:     SAMSCalculator::aTape                    Tape;
11:
12:     SAMSCalculator::aController              Calculator
13:     (
14:         ExternalInterface,
15:         Accumulator,
16:         Tape
17:     );
18:
19:     return Calculator.Operate();
20: }
```

ANALYSIS   Lines 8–10 define instances of the three classes needed by aController.

Lines 12–17 define an aController instance, naming it Calculator, and pass it the ExternalInterface, Accumulator, and Tape.

Line 19 runs the Calculator and returns any code it produces.

Summing Up

The section of the calculator implementation covered in this lesson has shown how to use the Standard C++ library vector class and how to isolate all contact with the outside world into anExternalInterface, and has changed the contents of main.cpp.

LESSON 21

Function and Operator Overloading

In this lesson, you will learn how you can have several functions with the same name in a class. You will also learn how to reimplement standard operators such as <<.

Declaring Overloaded Member Functions in a Class

The idea of *overloading* is to use the same name for more than one function in a class.

This can be useful when you have separate names for functions that do essentially the same thing, but differ only in the number or types of arguments required. For instance, anExternalInterface has member functions DisplayText(), DisplayRequest(), and DisplayNumber(). Wouldn't it be nice to be able to just call a function named Display() and have the compiler figure out which implementation to call based on the arguments provided?

C++ makes this fairly simple.

For instance, to the compiler, the following declarations represent separate and distinguishable member functions of anExternalInterface, despite having the same name:

```
void Display(const char *theText) const;
void Display(const aRequest &theRequest) const;
void Display(const float theNumber) const;
```

Once you have defined these, you can call them:

```
myExternalInterface.Display("Some text");
myExternalInterface.Display(theRequest);
myExternalInterface.Display(1.5);
```

These statements compile and run without compiler or runtime errors. Control flows to the correct implementations without any special work on your part.

Overloading is as simple as that. (At least, the basics are.)

> **How the Compiler Finds the Right Function** The compiler connects a member function call with its implementation by taking the class of the object, the name of the function called, and the sequence of the types of the actual arguments used in the function call (this is called the function call's *signature*). This call signature is checked against the implementation signature (the class, the name of the function, and the sequence of the types of the formal arguments for each implementation). The implementation whose signature *best* matches the signature of the call is the one that will be used.

The compiler's idea of the best match and your idea of the best match may not be the same if you have several functions that offer very similar argument types in the same order.

You have a few alternatives that can help keep your overloaded functions distinct. These will ensure that you get the results you expect:

- Try to make sure that your overloaded function argument types are as distinct as possible. For instance

```
void SomeFunction(const int theFirst, const int
➡theSecond, const long theThird);
```

and

```
void SomeFunction(const int theFirst, const long
theSecond, const int theThird);
```

are very similar and can be difficult to resolve for a call such as

```
SomeFunction(3,4,5);
```

In this situation, you might reconsider the overload and simply provide a "lowest common denominator" that can deal with int or long for any argument:

```
void SomeFunction(const long theFirst, const long
theSecond, const long theThird);
```

- You can change the order of arguments to make the overload distinct. For instance

```
void SomeFunction(const const int theFirst, const int
theSecond, char theThird);
void SomeFunction(const int theFirst, long theSecond,
char theThird);
```

could be replaced by

```
void SomeFunction(const int theFirst, const int
theSecond, char theThird);
void SomeFunction(char theThird, long theSecond, const
int theFirst);
```

This would force a caller of the second function to make the call distinct by placing the character as the first argument rather than the last.

- Keep the number of arguments low. One of the purposes of creating objects rather than procedural programs is to leverage the capability of the object to maintain internal state. There is nothing wrong with a sequence of calls such as

```
SomeObject.SetFirst(3);
SomeObject.SetSecond(4);
SomeObject.SetThird(5);
SomeObject.DoSomething();
```

or

```
SomeObject.SetFirst(3.2);
SomeObject.SetSecond("4.2");
SomeObject.SetThird(5);
SomeObject.DoSomething();
```

These calls leverage overloading as well as the capability of the object to maintain internal state. When DoSomething() is called, it works with whatever values have been set by prior function calls on the object.

Keep in mind that C++ does not use the function's return value type as part of the signature. Because of this, the following two declarations have the same signature and will cause a compiler error:

```
void Display(const char *theText) const;

int Display(const char *theText) const;
```

> **Overload Resolution**   The process of matching a function call signature with a function implementation/ definition. This process is also called *resolving*. In C++ this occurs at compile time; the compiler generates code to make the appropriate call or produces an error message if the call cannot be resolved.

Default arguments can cause problems for overloading. For instance, imagine two functions for anExternalInterface with these signatures:

```
void Display(const char *theText) const;
void Display
(
    const char *theText,
    const int thePadWidth = 12
) const;
```

The compiler will find it difficult to tell whether

```
ExternalInterface.Display("Stuff");
```

means to call

```
void Display(const char *theText) const;
```

or

```
void Display
(
    const char *theText,
    const int thePadWidth = 12
) const;
```

because the presence of a default value for the second argument leaves open the possibility that you intended to call the second function, but used only one argument. So the signature of the call matches both implementations.

The compiler will let you compile these functions into your class. However, when a program actually calls the function and only provides a literal string as an actual parameter, you get a compiler message that looks like this:

```
[C++ Error] Ambiguity between
'SAMSCalculator::anExternalInterface::Display
    (const char *) const' and
'SAMSCalculator::anExternalInterface::Display
    (const char *,const int) const'
```

Here, the compiler is telling you that it can't see the difference between the two functions (the overload is *ambiguous*). There is nothing you can do to change this except eliminate the default argument.

Instead of a default argument, provide these two functions:

```
void Display(const char *theText) const;

void Display
(
    const char *theText,
    const int thePadWidth
) const;
```

Have the first function assume a "PadWidth" of 12.

Overloaded Constructors

Prior to this lesson, you'd seen the use of overloading already—with the
constructor and copy constructor for aRequest (Lesson 17, "Classes:
Structures with Functions").

A constructor is a member function with a name that happens to be the
name of the class. Like any overloaded member function, it has a signature that the compiler uses for overload resolution. As with overloaded
functions, you shouldn't use default arguments for overloaded constructors.

What Does It Mean to Overload an Operator?

You have seen a variety of operators in C++, ranging from + and - to +=,
<<, and ++. Most of these operators have well-defined meanings and apply
to a fairly wide range of types, but none of them applies to user-defined
types such as structs and classes. This is not especially surprising. After
all, what does it mean to add two instances of aRequest together?

On the other hand, as you saw in the example that used std:string to
assemble messages for runtime_error (Lesson 11, "switch Statements,
static Variables, and runtime_errors"), it can be very convenient to
"add" two objects of a class together. The result in that case was a string
object that combined the two string objects from the right and left sides
of the + operator.

You've also seen the cout object overloading the insertion operator <<
(sometimes called the *left-shift operator*). This overloaded operator lets
you write statements such as

```
cout << "This" << Number << " is OK." << endl;
```

Finally, it can be useful to overload relational operators so that instances
of a class can be compared and sorted.

This style of coding is very natural for some classes. If you want to use it,
you need to overload operators. Almost every C++ operator is available
for overloading in your classes. All you need is to know how to do it.

Operator Overloading Can Be Dangerous

Operator overloading is one of the most overused and misused capabilities of C++. It is your responsibility to make sure that you do not misuse an operator symbol so that another programmer's intuitive understanding of what the operator means is violated. For instance, do not overload + to subtract, or reimplement ! to make a number negative. Also, you should clearly explain what any overloaded operator does by providing a comment where the operator is declared in the header file.

In general, your code is much more readable when you use conventional member functions with meaningful names rather than overloaded operators.

Overloading the << Operator

anExternalInterface might be somewhat easier to use if it offered the << operator, because you could then use anExternalInterface just as you use cout. For instance, you could write

myExternalInterface << "Presents: " << myTape.Element(Index);

You can add this capability fairly easily. Begin by declaring the operator << on const char * (that is, a C++ string literal) as a member of anExternalInterface, as shown in Listing 21.1.

LISTING 21.1   Overloading the << Operator in anExternalInterface

anExternalInterface &operator << (const char *theText);

Keep in mind that this is nothing magical; you are just declaring a function with an odd sort of name (operator <<).

ANALYSIS   The first part of this line is the type of the return value from the operator member function. Normally, you declare an operator member function to return a reference to an object of the class of which it is a member. In fact, an operator function should return a reference to the instance on which it was called.

This return value allows the next operator in a series to be applied to the same object as the first.

If anExternalInterface's Display() function were declared as

```
anExternalInterface &Display(const char *theText) const;
anExternalInterface &Display
    (const aRequest &theRequest) const;
anExternalInterface &Display(const float theNumber) const;
```

and each function returned the instance on which it was called, you could write

```
myExternalInterface.Display("Presents: ").
    ➡Display(myTape.Element(Index));
```

which would display

```
Presents: +34
```

Because the function operator << returns a reference to its instance, the following has the same effect:

```
myExternalInterface << "Presents: " << myTape.Element(Index);
```

Operator Member Functions Are Called Differently
Operator member functions don't use member selection operators to identify them as members of the class to their left, nor do they allow parentheses for their operand. The compiler recognizes these as function calls without such decorations. However, it is sometimes easier to understand operator function calls if you imagine them looking like regular calls. For instance:

```
myExternalInterface.<<("Presents: ").<<
    ➡(myTape.Element(Index));
```

This will not compile, but it conveys the meaning in a more familiar fashion.

The next item in the operator member function declaration is the special keyword operator, which tells the compiler that the name of the function is not a normal word, and that the compiler should look up the upcoming symbol in its table of operators. This will cause the compiler to make sure that the symbol is valid, and to determine how many arguments it should have. In this case, there is one argument—the text being provided.

The final part of the operator member function declaration is the argument to the operator function. In this case it is const char *, but it could be anything.

Operator Member Functions Have Zero or One Arguments Operator member functions overload either unary or infix operators. If the operator that you're overloading is unary (such as ! or ++), it has no arguments—it is applied directly to the class instance without any additional information needed. If the operator is infix (+, +=, <<, or !=), it has one argument, which must be of the type of the object expected on the right of the operator in an expression.

Because you can overload infix operator member functions, there can be several operator member functions declared for any operator, each with a different argument type.

By default, an overload of a unary operator that can be either prefix or postfix occurs on the prefix version. If you want to overload the postfix version, you need to provide a dummy argument. For instance, to overload the postfix increment operator, use the following:

```
aSomeClass &operator++(int theIgnored);
```

At this point you have completed the declaration of the overload of the << operator. Now you need to define it in the implementation file, as demonstrated in Listing 21.2.

LISTING 21.2   Implementing the << Operator in
anExternalInterface

```
1: anExternalInterface &anExternalInterface::operator <<
      ➥(const char *theText)
2: {
3:     Display(theText);
4:     return *this;
5: };
```

ANALYSIS Line 1 is the function implementation head, which is identical to the function prototype except that it contains *classname*:: before the function name (which is operator <<). As usual, this indicates that the function is a member of the class anExternalInterface.

Line 3 calls on the overloaded Display() function to cause the text to be displayed.

Line 4 returns a reference to the current instance of anExternalInterface. The special keyword this is a pointer to the instance of the object on which this function was called. * has its normal meaning, dereferencing the pointer so it can be assigned to a reference. Essentially, line 4 is equivalent to

```
anExternalInterface &ThisInstance = *this;
return ThisInstance;
```

You have now overloaded your first operator. You can create additional overloaded insertion operators for the other Display() functions:

```
anExternalInterface &operator << (const aRequest &theRequest);
anExternalInterface &operator << (const float theNumber);
```

You can also follow this pattern to overload other operators.

const and Overloaded Operators

Most of your member functions have been declared as const, but not the operator member function you just defined for anExternalInterface. Why not?

Normally, operators are created specifically to affect the state of the object on which they are called. But in the case of anExternalInterface, the insertion operator does not change its state. Therefore, we can and should make it const.

This is fairly simple in the function prototype—as usual, just add the const keyword to the end of the declaration.

In the implementation file, add const to the end of the function head.

There's only one slightly tricky thing, which you can see marked in the function definition shown in Listing 21.3.

LISTING 21.3   Making the << Operator const in anExternalInterface

```
1: anExternalInterface &anExternalInterface::operator <<
       ➡(const char *theText) const
2: {
3:     Display(theText);
*4:     return const_cast<anExternalInterface &>(*this);
5: };
```

ANALYSIS   Line 4 has to perform an unusual operation called const_cast on the result of *this. const_cast takes the non-const result of *this (a dereferenced pointer will never be const) and turns it into a const reference to anExternalInterface (as specified within the angle brackets).

Does this have any effect on the program or the object instance? No, its purpose is to satisfy the compiler. It means, "Yes, I the programmer know what I am doing, and I pledge that I have not changed this object in any detectable way, and I do not want the caller of the operator member function to think that I have."

Overloading Refresher

Remember the following key points:

- You can overload any function that has arguments.

- Simply declare, define, and use as many overloads of the function as you need variations in argument type, count, and order. But be careful—avoid having lots of arguments, try to keep the argument types very distinct, and, if all else fails, vary the order of argument types between the overloaded functions.

- The function return type does not change the function signature and cannot be used to distinguish between overloaded functions when the call is resolved.

- You can overload any operator, both unary (prefix or postfix) and infix.

- Unary operators can have a maximum of two overloads per class—one for prefix and one for postfix.

- Infix operators can have as many overloads as there are desired argument types, but no more, because they have only one argument.

- Wherever possible, avoid operator overloading. Use functions with readable names instead.

Overloading Assignment and the Copy Constructor

There is one area where nothing does the job better than operator overloading. You have seen the copy constructor and how it is used. As mentioned, it is typically only needed when member variables point to the heap. It is also only invoked when an object is explicitly or implicitly created as part of a copy (for instance, when a local variable is returned from a member function).

Assignment is not the same as copy creation—assignment can occur at any point in the life span of an object, not just at the beginning. For instance:

```
aRequest Request1(aRequest::add,34);
aRequest Request2(aRequest::multiply,22);
Request2 = Request1;
```

After the last statement, you expect Request2 to have an Operator() of aRequest::add and an Operand() of 34.

So, in addition to creating a copy constructor, you may need to overload the assignment operator—especially if you use heap-allocated storage for some of your member variables. As with the default copy constructor, default assignment does a member-by-member copy, which means that when you have heap-allocated members, assignment, like copying, will result in two objects sharing the same member data locations for those members.

It is important to avoid another issue that can occur in assignment: assigning an object to itself.

```
aRequest Request2(aRequest::multiply,22);
Request2 = Request2;
```

While this seems like a foolish mistake, in the presence of references and pointers, it is an easy one to make. As a cardinal rule, when you overload assignment operators, always make sure that you don't allow an object to be assigned to itself. If you aren't careful, a variety of difficult problems can result.

Listing 21.4 shows a sample assignment operator member function for aRequest, with an if statement to prevent the "foolish mistake."

LISTING 21.4   Overloading the = Operator in aRequest

```
 1: aRequest &operator = (aRequest &theOtherRequest)
 2: {
*3:     if (this != &theOtherRequest)
 4:     {
 5:         myOperator = theOtherRequest.myOperator;
 6:         myOperand = theOtherRequest.myOperator;
 7:     };
 8:
 9:     return *this;
10: }
```

ANALYSIS Line 3 checks to see whether theOtherRequest has the same location as this points to. If so, this is the same object as theOtherRequest, and the assignment is not performed.

It is a good idea to use an if statement like this in the copy constructor as well.

Summing Up

You have now seen how to create several functions with the same name and different argument types, and how the compiler supports overloading those names. In addition, you have seen that you can overload operators; this lesson has shown you how to overload the insertion and assignment operators, but you can overload many others.

You have seen some of the pitfalls of overloading and will hopefully be careful when you use this feature.

LESSON 22
Inheritance

In this lesson you will learn about inheritance—how to create a class that is based on another and then extended with new members and changed implementations to perform more specialized tasks.

Declaring Inheritance

Up until this lesson, you have been using C++ as an object-based language. To be truly object-oriented, a language must be able to support *inheritance*.

Inheritance is the ability to create a new class whose capabilities are based on at least one other class (often called the *superclass* or *ancestor*). Inheritance has been called "programming by difference," because the only code in the new class (called the *derived class* or *descendant*) is that which differs from the superclass.

Inheritance allows you to replace or add member functions or to add member variables to an existing class by creating a derived class and putting the changes in the new class. In most cases, you can do this without modifying the superclass.

You will practice inheritance in this lesson by extending the calculator classes. The extensions will restore the ability to stream out the tape at the end of the program run and to read it in at the start of the run.

The New and Changed Classes

The UML diagram of the calculator shown in Figure 22.1 (a revision of Figure 18.1) contains new and changed classes, indicated by the shaded boxes. The two new classes are aPersistentTape and aPersistentTapeExternalInterface. "Persistent" means "lasting."

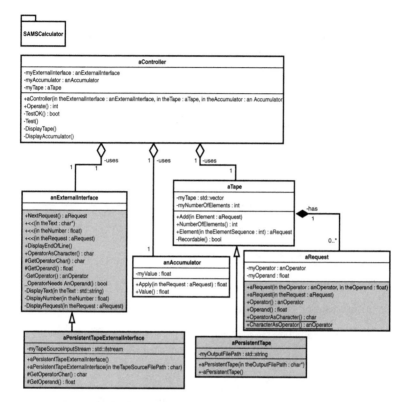

FIGURE 22.1 The UML class diagram with inheritance.

Changes have been made to the superclass anExternalInterface to get it ready to be used as the basis for aPersistentTapeExternalInterface. Also, some capabilities have been shifted from anExternalInterface to aRequest, in order to make the use of those capabilities by aPersistentTape and aPersistentTapeExternalInterface safer. These changes involved moving functions that translated aRequest::anOperator to and from a character into aRequest and will be discussed in Lesson 24, "Abstact Classes, Multiple Inheritance, and Static Members."

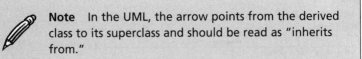

Note   In the UML, the arrow points from the derived class to its superclass and should be read as "inherits from."

Creating a Derived Tape Class

Inheritance is simple to declare. Listing 22.1 is the new declaration for aPersistentTape.

LISTING 22.1   aPersistentTape Header

```
 1: #ifndef PersistentTapeModuleH
 2: #define PersistentTapeModuleH
 3:
 4: #include <string>
 5:
*6: #include "TapeModule.h"
 7:
 8: namespace SAMSCalculator
 9: {
*10:    class aPersistentTape: public aTape
11:    {
12:       public:
13:
*14:          aPersistentTape(void);
*15:          aPersistentTape(const char *theOutputFilePath);
16:
*17:          ~aPersistentTape(void);
18:
19:       private:
20:
*21:          std::string myOutputFilePath;
22:    };
23: };
24:
25: #endif
```

ANALYSIS   Line 6 includes the declaration of the superclass aTape so that the compiler will know about its members when interpreting the declaration of aPersistentTape.

Line 10 declares that this class is based on aTape. This is indicated by the addition to the class declaration—: public aTape.

Line 14 *overrides* (replaces) the old constructor from aTape by naming a default constructor for this descendant.

Line 15 *overloads* (adds) a constructor that was not present in aTape. This new constructor saves theOutputFilePath, which will be used as the destination when writing the tape to a file; the path will be saved in myOutputFilePath.

Line 17 adds a destructor to the class. The tape will be written to the file when the instance is destroyed and this function is called.

Line 21 adds a new member variable, myOutputFilePath.

All the superclass constructors, functions, and member variables are part of this class as well. But none of them has to be mentioned in a descendant, unless they are overridden.

The Implementation of the Derived Class

You can see how this is implemented in Listing 22.2. The only code in the implementation is that which adds capabilities to the code in the superclass.

LISTING 22.2   aPersistentTape Implementation

```
 1: #include <fstream>
 2: #include <exception>
 3: #include <string>
 4:
*5: #include "PersistentTapeModule.h"
 6:
 7: namespace SAMSCalculator
 8: {
 9:     using namespace std;
10:
*11:     aPersistentTape::aPersistentTape(void)
*12:     {
*13:         throw
*14:             runtime_error
*15:             (
```

LISTING 22.2   Continued

```
 *16:                    string("The default constructor for
                           ➥aPersistentTape has been used. ") +
 *17:                    string("Use only the constructor that
                           ➥requires the file path.")
 *18:              );
 *19:    };
  20:
  21:    aPersistentTape::aPersistentTape
             ➥(const char *theOutputFilePath):
 *22:         myOutputFilePath(theOutputFilePath)
  23:    {
  24:    };
  25:
 *26:    aPersistentTape::~aPersistentTape(void)
 *27:    {
 *28:         if (myOutputFilePath.size() > 0)
 *29:         {
 *30:             ofstream OutputStream
                   ➥(myOutputFilePath.c_str(),ofstream::out);
 *31:
 *32:             int NumberOfTapeElements = NumberOfElements();
 *33:
 *34:             for
                   ➥(
                     ➥int Index = 0;
                     ➥Index < NumberOfTapeElements;
                     ➥Index++
                   ➥)
 *35:             {
 *36:                 OutputStream <<
                       ➥Element(Index).OperatorCharacter() <<
                       ➥Element(Index).Operand();
 *37:             };
 *38:         };
 *39:    };
  40: };
```

ANALYSIS Line 5 includes the header file for this class, as usual.

Lines 11–19 are designed to prevent anyone from using the default constructor. If the default constructor is used instead of the new constructor, it will throw an exception. This is needed because the superclass has a default constructor, and inheritance does not allow derived classes to eliminate anything they get from their ancestors. You cannot just get rid of aTape's default constructor; you have to hide it by overriding it.

Line 22 initializes the derived class member variable that holds the name of the file for output (myOutputFilePath) with the content of theOutputFilePath.

Lines 26–39 are the aPersistentTape destructor. This will be called when the instance goes out of scope, or, if the instance was created with new, when it is destroyed with delete. Line 32 uses the superclass member function NumberOfElements() to get the size of the tape. Line 36 uses the superclass member function Element() to write the specific element to the stream.

These calls to superclass member functions do not require any special keywords or other notation. Superclass members are part of the descendant and can be used just like any members actually declared in the descendant. The compiler knows where the functions come from and will find the correct implementation.

> **Watch Out When Overriding a Superclass Member**   If the descendant overrides a function in the superclass, a call in the descendant will, by default, call the override, not the superclass function. This can cause hard-to-find errors. Be careful.

There is one restriction on inheritance: You must use these functions rather than the member variable myTape, because myTape is a private variable of aTape, and private members of the superclass are hidden from any other class, even a derived class. This is actually a good thing, because it means that the superclass can be changed without changes to this class.

Referring to an Object as Its Class or Its Superclass

A look at the new `main.cpp` in Listing 22.3 shows that a reference to a superclass can refer to a descendant class as a result of inheritance.

LISTING 22.3   `main.cpp` Using the New Classes

```
 *1: #include "PersistentTapeExternalInterfaceModule.h"
  2: #include "AccumulatorModule.h"
 *3: #include "PersistentTapeModule.h"
  4: #include "ControllerModule.h"
  5:
  6: int main(int argc, char* argv[])
  7: {
 *8:     SAMSCalculator::aPersistentTapeExternalInterface
             ➥ExternalInterface(argv[1]);

  9:     SAMSCalculator::anAccumulator
             ➥Accumulator;

*10:     SAMSCalculator::aPersistentTape
             ➥Tape(argv[1]);
 11:
*12:     SAMSCalculator::aController
             ➥Calculator
*13:     (
*14:         ExternalInterface,
*15:         Accumulator,
*16:         Tape
*17:     );
 18:
 19:     return Calculator.Operate();
 20: }
```

ANALYSIS   Lines 1 and 3 include the new modules for the derived classes.

Lines 8 and 10 now define instances of `aPersistentTape` and `aPersistentTapeExternalInterface` in place of the old `aTape` and `anExternalInterface` variables. These variables use the special new constructors offered by the derived classes.

If you look back at Figure 22.1, you will notice that aController has not been changed. It still expects aTape and anExternalInterface references in its constructor's arguments, and it stores those references as member variables for use when Operate() is called.

This demonstrates a special feature of inheritance called *class polymorphism*. Class polymorphism means that a descendant class reference can be used anywhere a superclass reference can be used. For instance, an aPersistentTape object can be passed through an aTape reference argument and can be assigned to an aTape reference variable. As you will see, this does not mean that the object loses the capabilities added by the descendant. However, it does mean that those parts of the program that do not use the new public members of the derived class do not need to be changed. This reduces the risk of introducing errors during maintenance considerably.

Caution   Class polymorphism depends on the use of pointers or references. This is one of the reasons it is critical to avoid passing an actual class object as an argument and to avoid storing a copy of an instance. Where possible, use a reference.

Polymorphism   in C++, this refers to the ability to have many implementations with the same name. C++ supports three types of polymorphism: *method polymorphism* (overloaded functions), *operator polymorphism* (overloaded operators), and *class polymorphism*, which is the ability to reference a descendant class as if it were its superclass.

Class polymorphism works because a derived class can do everything a superclass can do—and more.

Levels of Inheritance

Keep in mind that there may be more than one level of derived class. C++ does not restrict the degree to which a class can be inherited, and it is not unusual for a mature class library to have four or five levels of classes inheriting from a superclass. In addition, more than one class can inherit from the same superclass. For this reason, programmers sometimes refer to the pattern of inheritance as the *inheritance tree*. It is an upside-down tree with the root at the top, as shown in Figure 22.2.

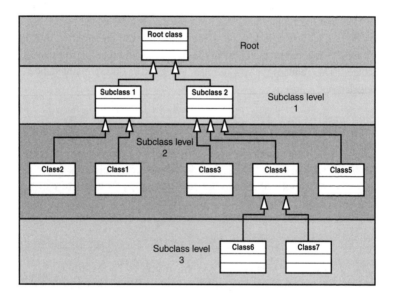

Figure 22.2   An inheritance tree.

Overriding Functions

As you've seen, a derived class can override the functions of its super-class. Member functions of the derived class can even call the functions of the superclass—including those implementations they are overriding. Figure 22.3 shows the possible variations.

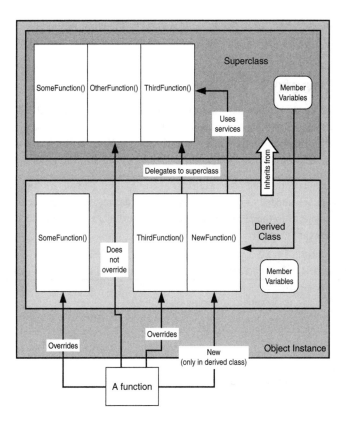

FIGURE 22.3   Calls to functions in a derived class.

This diagram shows an object instance, which consists of the derived class and its superclass. When a function outside the object calls on SomeFunction(), the call is handled completely by the derived class and is not passed on to the corresponding superclass implementation. When a function outside the object calls on OtherFunction(), because the derived class does not implement that function, the call is handled by the superclass implementation. When ThirdFunction() is called, it delegates the call to the superclass, and perhaps adds some of its own code to enhance the services provided by the superclass ThirdFunction(). Finally, NewFunction() is new in the derived class. It uses member variables (public member variables, of course) from the superclass and calls on

ThirdFunction() from the superclass as well (though it would be safer if
it called on the derived class implementation of ThirdFunction()).

Protected Access

As you've seen, a derived class cannot use member variables and functions declared in the private section of the superclass. But a superclass
can offer functions and member variables that only the superclass and its
derived classes can use, putting them in a special protected section.

The declaration of anExternalInterface in Listing 22.4 shows some of
the changes needed to make it ready for inheritance, including placing
two functions in the protected section so that they can be overridden by
aPersistentTapeExternalInterface.

LISTING 22.4   Protected Section in anExternalInterface

```
 1: #ifndef ExternalInterfaceModuleH
 2: #define ExternalInterfaceModuleH
 3:
 4: #include "RequestModule.h"
 5:
 6: namespace SAMSCalculator
 7: {
 8:     class anExternalInterface
 9:     {
10:       public:
11:
12:         anExternalInterface(void);
13:
14:         aRequest NextRequest(void) const;
15:
16:         anExternalInterface &operator <<
              ➥(const char *theText) const;
17:         anExternalInterface &operator <<
              ➥(const float theNumber) const;
18:         anExternalInterface &operator <<
              ➥(const aRequest &theRequest) const;
19:
20:         void DisplayEndOfLine(void) const;
21:
22:         char OperatorAsCharacter
              ➥(aRequest::anOperator theOperator) const;
```

LISTING 22.4   Continued

```
23:
*24:          protected:
*25:
*26:              virtual char GetOperatorChar(void);
*27:              virtual float GetOperand(void);
*28:
29:          private:
30:
31:              bool OperatorNeedsAnOperand
                    ➥(aRequest::anOperator theOperator) const;
32:              aRequest::anOperator GetOperator(void) const;
33:
34:              void Display(const char *theText) const;
35:              void Display(const aRequest &theRequest) const;
36:              void Display(const float theNumber) const;
37:      };
38: };
39:
40: #endif
```

ANALYSIS Lines 24–28 show the protected section. These are core functions for getting the operator character and the operand from the console, and they will be overridden in aPersistentTapeExternalInterface.

What Is `virtual`?

Lines 26 and 27 of Listing 22.4 show both functions qualified with the keyword `virtual`. This is important when functions are to be overridden, because it is the only way to make sure that class polymorphism works properly.

When a function outside an object calls a function in the object, the compiler generates code to perform the function call. If a function does not have the `virtual` keyword, the compiler assumes that the caller will want to call the function as implemented in the class the caller has at hand. Unfortunately, if the caller has a reference to a superclass of the class actually used to instantiate the object, and the derived class has overridden the function being called, the caller will not use the derived class's improved version of the function.

The keyword `virtual` tells the compiler that a function will be overridden in derived classes. The compiler prepares for this by performing any calls to that function through a function pointer. It maintains that function pointer to always point to the implementation of the function in the deepest derived class that overrode it.

This is especially powerful because it even works for calls from functions in the superclass to other member functions in the superclass. That is, a function in the superclass will end up calling the implementation of the function from the derived class if that function has the `virtual` keyword and if the instantiated object is actually of the derived class. That is exactly what the implementation of `aPersistentTapeExternalInterface` depends on.

Listing 22.5 shows one relevant section of the implementation of the superclass (`anExternalInterface`).

LISTING 22.5   GetOperatorChar() in Superclass anExternalInterface

```
 *1:    char anExternalInterface::GetOperatorChar(void)
 *2:    {
 *3:        char OperatorChar;
 *4:        cin >> OperatorChar;
 *5:        return OperatorChar;
 *6:    };
  7:
  8:    aRequest::anOperator
             ➥anExternalInterface::GetOperator(void) const
  9:    {
*10:        return aRequest::CharacterAsOperator
             ➥(GetOperatorChar());
 11:    };
```

ANALYSIS   Lines 1–6 are the superclass implementation of GetOperatorChar(). Line 10 calls GetOperatorChar(). But in Listing 22.6 from aPersistentTapeExternalInterface, GetOperatorChar() is overridden to first read from the tape file.

LISTING 22.6 GetOperatorChar() in Derived Class
aPersistentTapeExternalInterface

```
 1: char aPersistentTapeExternalInterface::GetOperatorChar
 2:    (void)
 3: {
 4:    if
 5:       (
 6:          myTapeSourceInputStream.is_open() &&
 7:          !myTapeSourceInputStream.eof()
 8:       )
 9:    {
10:       char OperatorChar;
11:       myTapeSourceInputStream >> OperatorChar;
12:
13:       if (OperatorChar == '\0') // The file is empty
14:       {
15:          myTapeSourceInputStream.close();
*16:          return anExternalInterface::GetOperatorChar();
17:       }
18:       else
19:       {
20:          return OperatorChar;
21:       };
22:    }
23:    else
24:    {
25:       if (myTapeSourceInputStream.is_open())
26:       {
27:          myTapeSourceInputStream.close();
28:       };
29:
*30:       return anExternalInterface::GetOperatorChar();
31:    };
32: };
```

ANALYSIS When, in the new implementation of main.cpp, main() gives
Calculator aPersistentTapeExternalInterface, and
Calculator calls myExternalInterface.NextRequest(), NextRequest()
calls anExternalInterface::GetOperator() which, as a result of
virtual, calls aPersistentTapeExternalInterface::
GetOperatorChar() rather than anExternalInterface::
GetOperatorChar(). This allows you to write only a very small amount of

very specific code in `aPersistentTapeExternalInterface` and reuse most of the code in `anExternalInterface`. In fact, on lines 16 and 30 of Listing 22.6, `aPersistentTapeExternalInterface` even delegates any need for input from the console to the superclass function implementation.

Virtual Constructors and Destructors

`virtual` is never used for constructors, but it is always a good idea for destructors. Otherwise, the superclass destructor may be called when a derived class is being destroyed through a superclass pointer or reference (by `delete`, in other words), and any storage allocated from the heap (or other resources claimed by the derived class) may not be disposed of properly. The fact that `aTape`'s destructor is `virtual` ensures that its descendants will be disposed of safely. Since "virtuality" is inherited, `aPersistentTape` has a virtual destructor courtesy of `aTape`.

Virtual Member Functions

`virtual` should always be used on a function in the protected section. If you envision a public function being overridden, it should also get the `virtual` keyword.

Some programmers worry about the performance penalty of the indirect `virtual` function call. In truth, this is probably not a significant drag on typical program performance, compared to things such as file I/O or database access, or even the time it takes to type a character.

Calling the Superclass

Line 30 of Listing 22.6 calls on `anExternalInterface`'s `GetOperatorChar()` when the tape file has run out of commands. Prefixing the function call with the name of the class where the function is defined followed by the scope resolution operator causes this to occur.

> **Referring to the Superclass Implementation Is Dangerous**   One of the most common problems in object-oriented systems where the inheritance tree evolves over time occurs when a new class is inserted into the tree between a derived class and its former superclass. If you were to insert such a class after making your call from the derived class to the superclass directly, as shown in Listing 22.6, you would then no longer be calling the real superclass function, but instead would be calling the super-superclass implementation. This is probably not what you want.
>
> Unfortunately, there is no compiler protection against this; it is simply a risk of maintenance. Use comments in the header file to alert others to the potential for this problem.

Summing Up

Inheritance is a very powerful but abstract feature. It primarily benefits programmers of larger systems that will evolve over time. As you have seen throughout this book, system enhancement, repair, and refactoring represent some of the most important activities programmers perform, far outweighing the time and effort spent on new programs and systems. So inheritance has a critical part to play in reducing the risk of introducing errors during maintenance and minimizing the effort needed to add new features.

You have seen how to create a derived class from a superclass, and how a reference to a superclass can end up with a call to derived class functions through the use of `virtual` (a feature called class polymorphism). You have learned about the need for virtual destructors and how `virtual` can allow even a superclass member function to call a derived class version of a superclass member function. You have also seen the variations in how functions are overridden.

You have seen inheritance in action and have seen a diagram of an inheritance tree. Once you have covered a few more topics, you will have completely mastered the core features of C++.

LESSON 23

Object Testing Using Inheritance

In this lesson, you will learn how classes and inheritance affect your ability to test C++ programs.

Writing Test Harnesses

You may recall the implementation of SelfTest(), which created an instance of anAccumulator and tested it. This is called a *test harness*. You can and should create a test harness for every class you implement.

The test harness can be a program, a part of an object, or an object itself, and often it will have a user interface. Test harnesses fall into several categories:

- Comprehensive—like SelfTest(), the test harness runs all the tests and checks the results against what is expected. A comprehensive test harness is especially good for quick regression tests. Some comprehensive test harnesses are driven by internal code, others by external files or databases.

- Front-end—the test harness runs all the tests but leaves it to a human to check the results.

- Manual—the test harness offers all the commands needed to run the tests, but leaves it to a human to decide which ones to run, in which order, and how to interpret the results. The calculator program itself can be considered a manual test harness for the SAMSCalculator::aController class and the objects it uses.

Testing the Classes with Known Cases

Tests fall into several categories as well:

- *Empty tests* determine whether a class, program, or system works correctly the first time it is run, or when it has no data. For instance, testing the most recent implementation of the calculator with an empty tape file shows that you need the following in aPersistentTapeExternalInterface:

```
 1:          char OperatorChar;
 2:          myTapeSourceInputStream >> OperatorChar;
 3:
*4:          if (OperatorChar == '\0')
 5:          {
 6:              myTapeSourceInputStream.close();
 7:              return anExternalInterface::
                      ➥GetOperatorChar();
 8:          }
 9:          else
10:          {
11:              return OperatorChar;
12:          };
```

An empty test reveals the need for Line 4; the empty file returns a char '\0', and when this character passes into the system it causes a bad operator exception. Adding an if statement prevents this problem.

- *Out-of-bounds tests* determine whether the class can handle results that are within the constraints of member function argument data types, but are outside the expected set of inputs to member functions.

- *Capacity (or stress) tests* determine how the class handles situations such as running out of memory. For instance, does it produce a reasonable error message before being stopped by the operating system or does it run amuck? You can use techniques such as repeating the use of operator new to allocate lots of memory. This will stress your system or program, but be aware that stress testing can be dangerous—it may cause an error that can crash your operating system or even do damage to your disk file structure. It is best to do such tests on a machine dedicated to the purpose.

- *Performance tests* determine how fast a program runs and where it is slow. A test harness can display the time before and after each test. Sometimes individual tests run so fast that a single test must be run thousands of times to get a noticeable number (for loops are useful in this case). Performance tests can also determine the performance profile of a program. For instance, how quickly does performance degrade as the tape gets larger? Does the tape size affect startup or shutdown most drastically, and when does it affect normal operations noticeably? Because C++ is often used in performance-critical applications, performance testing can be very important.

Keep in mind that even experienced programmers do not do a very good job guessing what will be slow in their programs. Performance tests are a good way to take a well-structured program and find out what is actually slowing it down.

There are tools called *profilers* that you can use to determine where a program spends its time. Such programs can produce reports on a class-by-class, function-by-function, or even line-by-line basis.

You can also profile your program by using ofstreams or cout to log the times at which various sections of your program start. Usually you need to use a very high-resolution timer for this purpose. Because the standard libraries don't provide such a timer, you will need to find a third-party class library that does.

It is a good idea to use "wolf fencing" (which was discussed in Lesson 14, "Testing") to zero in on performance problems. Whether using a profiler or your own profiling statements, start with the highest-level classes, focus on the slowest function, profile that, and repeat until you have isolated the part of the program that is slow.

- *Within-bounds tests* make sure that an object can handle expected inputs. Sometimes it can't. Randomly selected inputs are the most revealing in this kind of testing.

- *Boundary value tests* show whether an object has a problem with inputs that are right on the edge of acceptability. As with empty tests, these can often find errors that would otherwise only appear after a program has gone into the field.

Regression Testing

You have refactored the calculator several times on the journey to making it a full-fledged object-oriented program. Each time, you have been asked to run regression tests. Regression tests for the calculator have probably consisted of some set of requests that use all the operators. But in a professional situation, it is a good idea to run a fixed set of tests after each refactoring, repair, or enhancement.

Writing Test Inputs and Outputs to Files

Test harnesses can simplify the process of creating regression tests.

If you have a manual test harness, you can use it to prepare files for a comprehensive test harness. The manual test harness can prompt for inputs, record them, get the results, and prompt for confirmation that the results are correct. If results are correct, the inputs and results can be stored in separate files, to be read and reused at any time by a comprehensive test harness. In this way, manual and comprehensive test harnesses complement each other.

Using Inheritance

A derived class can be used to test a superclass. A derived class can be created solely to contain special methods to test public and protected methods of the superclass. In addition, class polymorphism enables a general test harness to test both a superclass and its subclasses—at least for features whose functions are declared in the superclass.

For instance, if you have the following inheritance:

```
class aFirstClass
{
...
};

class aSecondClass: public aFirstClass
{
...
};

class aTestHarness
{
    bool Test(aFirstClass &theFirstClass);
};
```

Then `TestHarness::Test()` can be used as follows:

```
aFirstClass A;
aSecondClass B;
aTestHarness TestHarness;
cout << "Test of A: " << TestHarness.Test(A) << endl;
cout << "Test of B: " << TestHarness.Test(B) << endl;
```

If `aSecondClass` overrides some of the functions of `aFirstClass`, those functions will be successfully tested by `Test()`. In addition, you can create a descendant of `aTestHarness` with a second `Test()` function that accepts an `aSecondClass` reference as a parameter instead of an `aFirstClass` reference. That member function can use the superclass `Test()` to test the `aFirstClass` part of `aSecondClass` and can have additional code to test any additional features added by `aSecondClass`.

Summing Up

Testing is a critical part of developing programs. Objects are loosely coupled to other objects and are very cohesive, making the object a natural unit for testing. You can test single objects or assemblies of objects, and there are many different types of test harnesses and tests.

The professional programming process often includes a quality assurance period during which non-programmers run regression tests on objects produced during development. This is not enough, however. Every programmer must be proficient in creating test harnesses and should consider building and using them a normal part of any programming effort.

LESSON 24

Abstract Classes, Multiple Inheritance, and Static Members

In this lesson you will learn how to create abstract classes to force derived classes to have certain members, how to inherit from several superclasses, and how to provide services from a class without requiring instantiation.

> **Note** The material in this lesson is considered advanced C++. If you have carefully followed the material in previous lessons, you should already be familiar with much of what you need to understand these concepts. Make sure to review Lesson 22, "Inheritance," in detail before tackling this lesson.

Creating Interfaces

Some classes have a lot of implementation. They essentially stand alone like little programs—self-contained and rich in capabilities. anAccumulator is such a class.

Other classes provide a basic implementation for their descendants to extend in a general way. aTape is such a class.

Still others are designed to leverage virtual functions so that a specific feature can be extended or changed. anExternalInterface is such a class. It calls on certain of its own member functions that are intended to be overridden or extended by a descendant class.

Finally, some classes declare functions, but do not implement them, leaving implementation to their descendants. Such classes, often called *interfaces* or *abstract classes*, are intended as guidelines for programmers, indicating what should be implemented in their descendants.

Let's look at abstract classes in more detail.

Pure Virtual Functions

The term *pure virtual functions* is a mouthful, but such functions are essential to creating abstract classes. They provide a way to declare functions that offer no implementation.

Let's start with the "virtual" part. You may recall from Lesson 22 that the keyword `virtual` allows a function call to connect with the appropriate implementation, even when a reference to a superclass is used to make the call. The compiler calls a virtual function indirectly through a function pointer stored in the object.

You can make a virtual function "pure" (that is, "uncontaminated by any implementation") by initializing its function pointer to zero:

```
virtual char GetOperatorChar(void) = 0;
```

A pure virtual function is usually called *abstract*. Because of this, any class with one or more pure virtual functions is called an *abstract class*. You are not allowed to instantiate an object of an abstract class because your program would crash if you called any of its pure virtual member functions. Trying to instantiate an abstract class will cause a compiler error message.

Putting a pure virtual function in your class tells other programmers two things about your class:

- They can't instantiate an object of this class—they should create a descendant class from it.

- They must override all pure virtual functions in the descendant class, or they will not be able to instantiate the descendant class.

Class polymorphism, which lets you refer to an object as if it were an instance of its superclass, lets you use pointers and references that appear to refer to instances of abstract classes. But these must actually point to or reference instances of *concrete* descendant classes. Calls to member functions declared in the abstract class will reach their concrete class implementations as a result of those functions being virtual.

> **Concrete Classes**   The opposite of an abstract class, a concrete class has no pure virtual member functions, whether in its own declaration or inherited from its superclasses. Most classes are concrete classes. A class whose superclass is abstract will only be concrete when it implements every pure virtual function from the superclass.

An Abstract Class Declaration

It is often useful to create abstract classes as the root of your inheritance tree. This allows other programmers to create classes to work with your abstract class—even when you haven't yet created any concrete descendant classes.

In a large development project, abstract classes make it easier for everyone to work simultaneously on different parts of the system, and to later bring all classes together for *integration* into a complete program. Abstract classes let programmers use the compiler to ensure that there will be no mismatches in function names or signatures between caller and callee, even when different programmers develop the caller and callee.

Though a little late in this programming project, you can create abstract classes for the calculator.

Take, for example, anAccumulator, currently the only type of accumulator in our system. To create an abstract class that you can use to represent any type of accumulator, you can refactor the original class and make anAccumulator abstract. The accumulator implementation can then be moved into a descendant class, called aBasicAccumulator. Listing 24.1 shows a new header for anAccumulator.

LISTING 24.1   anAccumulator Header, Now an Abstract
Class Declaration

```
 1: #ifndef AccumulatorModuleH
 2: #define AccumulatorModuleH
 3:
 4: #include "RequestModule.h"
 5:
 6: namespace SAMSCalculator
 7: {
 8:     class anAccumulator
 9:     {
10:         public:
11:
*12:             anAccumulator(void);
*13:             anAccumulator(anAccumulator &theAccumulator);
*14:             virtual ~anAccumulator(void);
15:
*16:             virtual float Apply
                      ➥(const aRequest &theRequest) = 0;
*17:             virtual float Value(void) const = 0;
18:
*19:             virtual anAccumulator
                      ➥&ReferenceToANewAccumulator(void) = 0;
20:
21:         protected:
22:
*23:             float myValue;
24:     };
26: };
27:
28: #endif
```

ANALYSIS   Lines 12 and 13 declare the constructor and copy constructor. Constructors are needed because anAccumulator still has
a member variable declared: myValue on line 23. The constructors will initialize myValue. They are the only member functions of this class to have
an implementation.

myValue has been moved to the protected section, so the descendant
classes that will implement anAccumulator's abstract functions can make
use of myValue. Remember, even descendant classes cannot access private
members.

Descendant classes will be able to depend on anAccumulator initializing myValue to 0.

Line 14 is the virtual destructor. Every class destined for inheritance should have a virtual destructor.

Lines 16 and 17 are the accumulator functions changed to pure virtual functions by the addition of the virtual keyword at the start of the prototype and the = 0 at the end.

Line 19 defines a new function, ReferenceToANewAccumulator(). That function returns a reference to an object of the abstract class anAccumulator. You will see how this works (and why we need it) later in this lesson.

Implementing the Abstract Class

What used to be the class anAccumulator is implemented by the descendant class aBasicAccumulator, shown in Listing 24.2. You can see that the class header for aBasicAccumulator looks the same as the one for anAccumulator used to, except that myValue has been removed and ReferenceToANewAccumulator() has been added. These changes are needed because myValue is provided by the superclass, and because ReferenceToANewAccumulator() must be implemented here to make aBasicAccumulator into a concrete class.

LISTING 24.2   aBasicAccumulator Header, Now Representing the Implementation of anAccumulator

```
 1: #ifndef BasicAccumulatorModuleH
 2: #define BasicAccumulatorModuleH
 3:
 4: #include "AccumulatorModule.h"
 5: #include "InstanceCountableModule.h"
 6:
 7: namespace SAMSCalculator
 8: {
 9:     class aBasicAccumulator: public anAccumulator
10:     {
11:        public:
12:
13:            aBasicAccumulator(void);
14:            aBasicAccumulator
                    ➡(aBasicAccumulator &theAccumulator);
```

LISTING 24.2   Continued

```
15:
16:          float Apply(const aRequest &theRequest);
17:          float Value(void) const;
18:
19:          anAccumulator &ReferenceToANewAccumulator(void);
20:    };
21: };
22:
23: #endif
```

Changes to aController

anAccumulator is now abstract and cannot be instantiated, so aController::SelfTest() can no longer use the following statement without a compiler error:

```
anAccumulator TestAccumulator;
```

To allow for the future use of different types of accumulators with aController, aController::SelfTest() should get its instance of anAccumulator through the ReferenceToANewAccumulator() member function of its myAccumulator member variable.

If SelfTest() simply created and tested an instance of aBasicAccumulator, SelfTest() would need to be modified each time you decided to use a different accumulator class with aController. Using ReferenceToANewAccumulator() places the responsibility for providing the right class of accumulator in the hands of the concrete descendant of anAccumulator that was passed to this instance of aController, and insulates aController from changes in the type of accumulator provided to it.

The call to ReferenceToANewAccumulator() is shown in Listing 24.3.

LISTING 24.3   SelfTest Getting an Instance of aBasicAccumulator from myAccumulator. ReferenceToANewAccumulator()

```
  1:     void aController::SelfTest(void) const
  2:     {
 *3:          anAccumulator &TestAccumulator =
                 ↪myAccumulator.ReferenceToANewAccumulator();
```

LISTING 24.3   Continued

```
 4:
 5:        try
 6:        {
 7:            if
 8:                (
 9:                    TestOK(TestAccumulator,aRequest
                           ➡(aRequest::add,3),3) &&
10:                    TestOK(TestAccumulator,aRequest
                           ➡(aRequest::subtract,2),1) &&
11:                    TestOK(TestAccumulator,aRequest
                           ➡(aRequest::multiply,4),4) &&
12:                    TestOK(TestAccumulator,aRequest
                           ➡(aRequest::divide,2),2)
13:                )
14:            {
15:                cout << "Test OK." << endl;
16:            }
17:            else
18:            {
19:                cout << "Test failed." << endl;
20:            };
21:        }
22:        catch (...)
23:        {
24:            cout << "Test failed because of an exception.";
25:        };
26:
*27:        delete &TestAccumulator;
28:    };
```

ANALYSIS   Line 3 uses ReferenceToANewAccumulator() to get a
TestAccumulator from the member variable object
myAccumulator.

SelfTest() expects a reference to anAccumulator. If it were actually able
to get an instance of anAccumulator, it would crash the first time a member function of TestAccumulator was called. But, unknown to
SelfTest(), ReferenceToANewAccumulator() actually returns a reference
to a heap-allocated instance of aBasicAccumulator, which can be safely
used by SelfTest() thanks to virtual functions and class polymorphism.

Line 27 deletes the storage for TestAccumulator.

An Object Factory

So how does this work? Here's how aBasicAccumulator implements
ReferenceToANewAccumulator():

```
1:      anAccumulator &aBasicAccumulator::
            ➥ReferenceToANewAccumulator(void)
2:      {
3:          return *(new aBasicAccumulator);
4:      };
```

ANALYSIS   Line 3 creates an instance of aBasicAccumulator with new
and then dereferences that pointer in the return statement—
this is normal when returning a reference to an object.

The reference to be returned is to an instance of aBasicAccumulator, not
to an instance of anAccumulator. But because aBasicAccumulator is a
descendant of anAccumulator, the compiler doesn't complain. Once
again, class polymorphism makes things easier for you.

ReferenceToANewAccumulator() is an example of an *object-oriented programming pattern* called a *factory*. *Object-oriented patterns* (often called
"OO patterns," pronounced "oh oh patterns") are a hot topic among
object-oriented programmers in all languages and there are several books
documenting the various patterns that have been developed.

The factory pattern allows an abstract class to appear to provide instances
of itself, while actually requiring that a concrete descendant class provide
instances of its class instead.

Abstract Classes in the Inheritance Tree

Abstract classes are usually the root classes of inheritance trees, as Figure
24.1 shows.

The use of abstract classes makes it easier for a team of class programmers to work separately on the classes needed for a program such as
SAMSCalculator. Even if your classes depend on abstract classes whose
implementation is assigned to other programmers, you can create and
compile your program with nothing more than the abstract classes provided at the beginning of your project. Of course, you will need either
their concrete classes or your own (probably simplified) concrete classes

to actually run a test. Such classes are often called *stubs* or *simulators* and their member functions can simply display a message indicating that they have been called, or can return very simple, preprogrammed results.

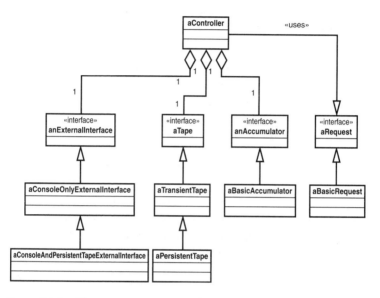

FIGURE 24.1   The SAMSCalculator inheritance tree with abstract classes.

As each class programmer completes a concrete class, an integration programmer can combine it with others into a complete program. When class programmers use abstract classes, stubs, and test harnesses, the chances are excellent that the first run after integration will be successful. And because the class programmers are able to work separately and in parallel, the program can be completed several times faster than if a single programmer were responsible for everything.

Multiple Inheritance

C++ allows a class to inherit from more than one superclass using a feature called *multiple inheritance*. Multiple inheritance is a controversial feature that always provokes strong arguments. Many programmers believe that multiple inheritance is not only unnecessary but even danger-ous—though there are probably just as many who think it is an essential tool and that it can be used wisely.

Inheritance represents a relationship between classes often called "is a." For instance, `aPersistentTapeExternalInterface` is `anExternalInterface` with additional features.

Aggregation, the use of objects as member variables, as `aController` uses `anAccumulator`, represents a relationship between instances called "has" (when the instance owns the members) or "uses" (when the instance shares the members). It would not be correct to say `aController` *is* `anAccumulator`. It *uses* an instance of `anAccumulator`.

> **Caution** Many programmers use multiple inheritance when they should use aggregation. This is a major cause of the controversy over multiple inheritance. But with proper understanding of the difference between *is a* and *uses/has*, you can use multiple inheritance safely.

Multiple inheritance *can* be useful. For instance, you might wish to add an instance count to all your classes to find out how many objects have been instantiated at any point in time. You can do so by creating an `isInstanceCountable` class and ensuring that all your classes inherit it. (The prefix "is" indicates that `isInstanceCountable` adds capabilities to existing classes through multiple inheritance.) Figure 24.2 shows this change.

Multiple inheritance will require a change to the declaration of each class to be made "instance countable." Listing 24.4 shows `aBasicAccumulator` with these changes.

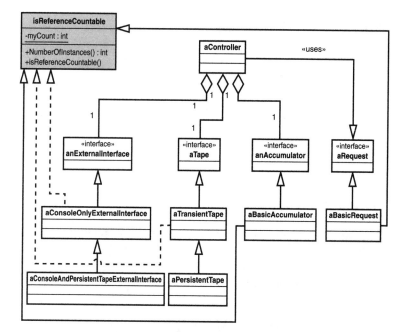

FIGURE 24.2 The SAMSCalculator inheritance tree with abstract classes and multiple inheritance.

LISTING 24.4 Header for aBasicAccumulator Showing Multiple Inheritance

```
 1: #ifndef BasicAccumulatorModuleH
 2: #define BasicAccumulatorModuleH
 3:
 4: #include "AccumulatorModule.h"
*5: #include "InstanceCountableModule.h"
 6:
 7: namespace SAMSCalculator
 8: {
*9:     class aBasicAccumulator:
10:         public anAccumulator,public isInstanceCountable
11:     {
12:         public:
13:
```

LISTING 24.4   Continued

```
14:            aBasicAccumulator(void);
15:
16:            aBasicAccumulator
17:               (aBasicAccumulator &theAccumulator);
18:
19:            float Apply(const aRequest &theRequest);
20:            float Value(void) const;
21:
22:            anAccumulator &ReferenceToANewAccumulator(void);
23:    };
24: };
25:
26: #endif
```

ANALYSIS   The only changes are line 5 (the #include for the header of the additional superclass) and line 9, which identifies the two superclasses. You can see that multiple inheritance simply lists public *classname* for each superclass, separated by commas.

Static Member Variables and Functions in Classes

A quick look at main() in Listing 24.5 shows how it uses the instance-counting feature.

LISTING 24.5   Main.cpp Using
isInstanceCountable::TotalNumberOfInstances()

```
 1: #include <iostream>
 2:
 3: #include
    ➥"ConsoleAndPersistentTapeExternalInterfaceModule.h"
 4: #include "BasicAccumulatorModule.h"
 5: #include "PersistentTapeModule.h"
 6: #include "ControllerModule.h"
 7: #include "InstanceCountableModule.h"
 8:
 9: using namespace std;
10:
```

LISTING 24.5   Continued

```
11: int main(int argc, char* argv[])
12: {
13:     SAMSCalculator::
              aConsoleAndPersistentTapeExternalInterface
14:           ExternalInterface(argv[1]);
15:
16:     SAMSCalculator::aBasicAccumulator    Accumulator;
17:     SAMSCalculator::aPersistentTape      Tape(argv[1]);
18:
19:     SAMSCalculator::aController          Calculator
20:     (
21:         ExternalInterface,
22:         Accumulator,
23:         Tape
24:     );
25:
*26:    int ResultCode = Calculator.Operate();
27:
*28:    cout <<
*29:        "Total instances of all classes: " <<
*30:        SAMSCalculator::isInstanceCountable::
              TotalNumberOfInstances() <<
*31:        endl;
32:
*33:    char PauseCharacter;
*34:    cin >> PauseCharacter;
35:
*36:    return ResultCode;
37: }
```

ANALYSIS   Line 26 now defines a variable for the return code from Calculator.Operate(). This is needed so that main() does not return immediately when Operate() is complete, and provides an opportunity to display the instance count.

Line 30 uses *namespace*::*classname*::*functionname* notation to get the count of all the instances of all the SAMSCalculator classes in existence at that point.

But how is that count generated? And how can we get the instance count from isInstanceCountable without having an instance of that class?

`static` in a Class

You might remember using static variables when `Tape()` and `Accumulator()` were functions. In that context, the `static` variable was a variable initialized when the program started and whose value was retained between function calls.

You abandoned that type of variable when you refactored the calculator into classes because class member variables allowed the accumulator and the tape to retain internal state, just as the static variable used to.

However, the static variable can still play a role in classes. A static variable in a class is initialized when the program starts and is shared between all instances of the class. You can use such a variable to hold the total count of the `SAMSCalculator` classes.

Listing 24.6 is the declaration of `isInstanceCountable`, showing the variable that counts the instances.

LISTING 24.6   Declaration of `isInstanceCountable`

```
 1: #ifndef InstanceCountableModuleH
 2: #define InstanceCountableModuleH
 3:
 4: namespace SAMSCalculator
 5: {
 6:     class isInstanceCountable
 7:     {
 8:         public:
 9:
10:             isInstanceCountable(void);
11:             ~isInstanceCountable(void);
12:
*13:            static int TotalNumberOfInstances(void);
14:
15:         private:
16:
*17:            static int ourInstanceCounter;
18:
19:     };
20:
21: };
22:
23: #endif
```

ANALYSIS Line 17 is a static int that is shared by all instances of the isInstanceCountable class. The name is prefixed with "our" to remind you that this is a *class-level variable.*

If you instantiate three objects of this class, ourInstanceCounter will have a value of 3. You will see how this is done when you look at the constructor implementation for this class.

Because each SAMSCalculator class inherits from this class as well as from its interface, all SAMSCalculator classes share this variable.

Line 13 is a *static function.* static applied to a member function means that you can call the function without an instance of the class. A static function is also referred to as a *class function*, because you call it using the classname and the scope resolution operator (*classname*:: *functionname*()), or, in this case, *namespacename*::*classname*:: *functionname*()). Line 30 of main() calls this function.

Incrementing and Decrementing the Instance Count

The constructor and destructor of isReferenceCountable, shown in Listing 24.7, increment and decrement ourInstanceCounter.

LISTING 24.7   Implementation of isInstanceCountable

```
1: #include "InstanceCountableModule.h"
2:
3: namespace SAMSCalculator
4: {
5:     int isInstanceCountable::ourInstanceCounter = 0;
6:
7:     isInstanceCountable::isInstanceCountable(void)
8:     {
9:         ourInstanceCounter++;
10:    };
11:
12:    isInstanceCountable::~isInstanceCountable(void)
13:    {
14:        ourInstanceCounter--;
15:    };
16:
```

LISTING 24.7   Continued

```
17:     int isInstanceCountable::TotalNumberOfInstances(void)
18:     {
19:         return ourInstanceCounter;
20:     };
21:
22: };
```

ANALYSIS   Line 5 initializes the static counter variable
ourInstanceCounter. This occurs when the program starts
and is not connected with any instance of the class. Line 5 is called a *static initializer*.

Lines 7–10 increment the counter when an instance of this class is created. With multiple inheritance, when a descendant class is instantiated, the constructors of all its superclasses are called—which means that any instantiation of a class that inherits from isInstanceCountable will increment ourInstanceCounter.

Lines 12–15 decrement the counter when an instance of this class is destroyed. As with constructors, destructors for superclasses are called when a derived class is destroyed.

As a result, the counter keeps track of every class as it is created and destroyed.

Remember to Use Virtual Destructors

isInstanceCountable instance counting will not work properly if the SAMSCalculator classes do not have virtual destructors. You should declare a virtual destructor for each interface class. This is required so that the destruction of the classes through an abstract class reference (as happens in SelfTest()) will call the correct destructor rather than just the destructor for the abstract class.

The Output of `main.cpp`

Here is the result of running the updated calculator. Because the calculator just accepts input without a prompt, there is no prompt shown:

INPUT   `+3-2*4/2=`

OUTPUT   2

INPUT   !

OUTPUT

```
+ - OK.
- - OK.
* - OK.
/ - OK.
Test OK.
```

INPUT   .

OUTPUT   `Total instances of all classes: 8`

Did this work correctly? If you look in `main()`, you will see four classes instantiated: `aController`, `aBasicAccumulator`, `aConsoleAndPersistentTapeExternalInterface`, and `aPersistentTape`. This represents four of the eight instances shown.

In addition, the user enters four calculations, each of which generates one `aRequest` instance for the tape, creating a total of four more instances, bringing the grand total to eight. Also note that if you had not declared a virtual destructor in `anAccumulator`, the count would be 9, because the `isInstanceCountable` destructor would not have been called when `SelfTest()` deleted `TestAccumulator`. Remember, `isInstanceCountable` is inherited by `aBasicAccumulator`, not by its superclass `anAccumulator`.

Summing Up

This lesson has presented some very advanced C++ material, including the declaration of pure abstract functions, abstract versus concrete classes, the role of interfaces in the inheritance tree, the uses and abuses of multiple inheritance, and the role of static variables and functions in classes.

LESSON 25
Templates

In this lesson, you will learn to declare and define templates. Templates enable you to build classes that work with a variety of types without having to rewrite the class for every type.

Strengths and Weaknesses of Templates

Picking the data type or class that will be at the core of your program or class can be difficult.

For instance, the calculator used `int`s until it was revealed that there were arithmetic problems as a result of that choice. You might recall from Lesson 4, "Numeric Input," that changing the calculator to use `float`s instead of `int`s forced modifications affecting almost every part of the code.

Changing the object-oriented calculator to use `long double` instead of `float` for greater accuracy would be no different: It would require changes in every class. And if you wanted to have an `int` calculator, a `float` calculator, and a `long double` calculator all at the same time, you might have to reimplement the classes used by the calculator several times.

Templates make it possible to avoid these far-reaching changes and multiple implementations.

Declaring and Using Templates

You've seen a template in use before—`std::vector<aRequest> myTape;` in `aTape`, from Lesson 20, "The Rest of the Calculator as Classes." This member variable declaration created an instance of vector that would only accept aRequest objects.

It can help to think of such a template as a form that will generate code for a class when you "fill in the blanks."

Templates usually have only one or at most a few such "blanks," which are called *type parameters*. A value supplied for the type parameter is used to replace that type parameter wherever it is mentioned in the template. In std::vector<aRequest>, aRequest is the value supplied for the type parameter of the vector template.

The format for coding a template can seem complex but is actually fairly simple. There are basically two parts to a template class, as with any class: a declaration and a definition.

A template declaration adds template <class ofType> to the start of the normal class declaration. This identifies the name for the type parameter and tells the compiler that the class is a template class.

A template definition (the implementation of the template class) adds template <class ofType> to the start of each member function definition head and <ofType> follows the classname in that header (to tell the compiler that the function is a member of the template class).

Here is an example of a template header file, where ofType is the type parameter:

```
#include <whatever>
namespace SomeNamespace
{
    template <class ofType> class aSampleTemplate
    {
        public:
            ofType SomeFunction
                (int theArgument, ofType theOther Argument);
    };

    template <class ofType> ofType
        aSampleTemplate<ofType>::SomeFunction
            (int theArgument, ofType theOtherArgument)
    {
        int Thing = theArgument;
```

```
        ofType OtherThing = theOtherArgument;
        return OtherThing;
    };
};
```

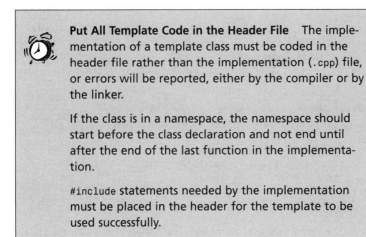

Put All Template Code in the Header File   The implementation of a template class must be coded in the
header file rather than the implementation (.cpp) file,
or errors will be reported, either by the compiler or by
the linker.

If the class is in a namespace, the namespace should
start before the class declaration and not end until
after the end of the last function in the implementation.

#include statements needed by the implementation
must be placed in the header for the template to be
used successfully.

When you define a variable using this template with float for the type
parameter ofType, as in

```
aSampleTemplate<float> SampleThing;
```

the compiler will internally generate a class declaration and implementation based on the provided type. This is called *specialization*.

Specialization   Instantiating an object from a template. The template is said to be *specialized* when an
actual type is used for the type parameter. For
instance, std::vector<aRequest> is the template class
std::vector specialized for the aRequest type.

Here is what such a generated class might look like if you could see it
(the class is both generated and given a name "behind the scenes" by the

compiler—in this case, the name is the type parameter value followed by the template classname floataSampleTemplate):

```
#include <whatever>
namespace SomeNamespace
{
    class floataSampleTemplate
    {
        public:
            float SomeFunction
                (int theArgument, float theOther Argument);
    };

    float aSampleTemplateFloat::SomeFunction
        (int theArgument, float theOtherArgument)
    {
        int Thing = theArgument;
        float OtherThing = theOtherArgument;
        return OtherThing;
    };
};
```

This class is never visible in your code—the compiler generates the class as it processes your program. However, the compiler treats the generated class just as it would treat any class you had written directly into the program source code.

From the compiler's point of view, the variable definition

```
aSampleTemplate<float> SampleThing;
```

is changed to reference the internal classname the compiler generates:

```
floataSampleTemplate SampleThing
```

Again, this is never visible to you—it happens completely behind the scenes.

The Calculator as Templates

Let's apply templates to the calculator. Listing 25.1 shows the declaration of aRequest turned into a template.

LISTING 25.1   aRequest Declared as a Template Class

```
 *1:    template <class ofType> class aRequest:
 *2:        public isInstanceCountable
  3:    {
  4:        public:
  5:
  6:            // Note: There is no default constructor -
  7:            // you must provide an operator and operand when
  8:            // creating an instance of this class
  9:
*10:            aRequest
*11:            (
*12:                const anOperator theOperator,
*13:                const ofType anOperand
*14:            );
 15:
 16:            // Allow a copy
 17:
 18:            aRequest(const aRequest &theOtherRequest);
 19:
 20:            // Support assignment
 21:
 22:            aRequest &operator =
 23:                (const aRequest &theOtherRequest);
 24:
 25:            // These can be called without an instance:
 26:
 27:            static char OperatorAsCharacter
 28:                (const anOperator theOperator);
 29:
 30:            static anOperator CharacterAsOperator
 31:                (const char theCharacter);
 32:
 33:            // You cannot change the operator or operand
 34:            // after an instance of this class is created;
 35:            // you can only get their values
 36:
 37:            anOperator Operator(void) const;
 38:            char OperatorCharacter(void) const;
 39:
*40:            ofType Operand(void) const;
 41:
 42:        private:
 43:
```

LISTING 25.1   Continued

```
44:             anOperator myOperator;
*45:            ofType myOperand;
46:     };
```

ANALYSIS This listing shows only the declaration part of the header file. The implementation of a template will also be in the header file. This is required so that the compiler can generate the appropriate implementation at compile time, based on the type parameter. The implementation file for aRequest (the file RequestModule.cpp) will now only contain a #include of its header file. (ISO/ANSI C++ requires some code in the implementation file and the #include of the header is the minimum you can provide.)

The template class implementation must immediately follow the class declaration in the header file.

The declaration of the enumerated type anOperator has been moved out of declaration for aRequest. The compiler I used while writing this book cannot find that type nested within this template class, so certain expressions elsewhere in the program (such as aRequest<float>::add) cause an error. Your compiler may or may not experience such problems with type declarations nested in templates. Keep in mind that templates are a comparatively new feature and there is some variation in how well compilers handle them.

Lines 1 and 2 are the new class declaration head, showing that the type parameter is called ofType.

Lines 10–14 declare the constructor for the class, with the use of the type parameter to stand in for the type of the argument theOperand on line 13.

Line 40 uses the type parameter to stand in for the type of the return value of the Operand() function.

Line 45 declares the myOperand member variable, again using ofType to stand in for its type.

Listing 25.2 shows the effect of being part of a template on the definition of the constructor for this class. Remember, this definition is inside the namespace declaration that wraps the header file, and is only one of several function definitions that follow the class declaration.

LISTING 25.2   aRequest Constructor in the Template Header File

```
*1:    template <class ofType> aRequest<ofType>::aRequest
 2:    (
 3:        const anOperator theOperator,
*4:        const ofType theOperand
 5:    ) :
 6:        myOperator(theOperator),
*7:        myOperand(theOperand)
 8:    {
 9:    };
```

ANALYSIS   Line 1 identifies this as a function that uses the type parameter ofType and is a member of the class aRequest<ofType>.

Line 4 uses the type parameter to stand for the type of the incoming argument to the constructor.

Line 7 initializes the member variable. You will notice that this line is the same as it was in previous, non-template versions of the constructor.

Listing 25.3 shows the Operand() function, which is only slightly affected by being in a template.

LISTING 25.3   aRequest Member Function Operand() in the Template Header File

```
*1:    template <class ofType>
*2:        ofType aRequest<ofType>::Operand(void) const
 3:    {
*4:        return myOperand;
 5:    };
```

ANALYSIS   Line 1 identifies this member function as being part of a template and shows that the type parameter name is ofType.

Line 2 is the function header, with the return type specified as whatever type has been provided in the type parameter.

Line 4 returns the member variable value and is unchanged from previous versions of the program.

Changing **anAccumulator** and **aBasicAccumulator**

You might recall that in Lesson 24, "Abstract Classes, Multiple Inheritance, and Static Members," the class anAccumulator was made abstract, and aBasicAccumulator was made into the implementation class. Both classes will need to be made templates so that they can work with aRequest<ofType>.

anAccumulator, because it is an abstract class, has a very small implementation, so its header file is simple, as shown in Listing 25.4.

LISTING 25.4   anAccumulator Template Header File

```
 1: #ifndef AccumulatorModuleH
 2: #define AccumulatorModuleH
 3:
*4: #include "RequestModule.h"
 5:
 6: namespace SAMSCalculator
 7: {
*8:     template <class ofType> class anAccumulator
 9:     {
10:        public:
11:
12:            anAccumulator(void);
13:            anAccumulator(anAccumulator &theAccumulator);
14:
15:            virtual ~anAccumulator(void);
16:
*17:           virtual ofType Apply
*18:              (const aRequest<ofType> &theRequest) = 0;
19:
*20:           virtual ofType Value(void) const = 0;
21:
22:            virtual anAccumulator
23:               &ReferenceToANewAccumulator(void) = 0;
24:
25:        protected:
26:
*27:           ofType myValue;
28:     };
29:
30:     using namespace std;
```

LISTING 25.4   Continued

```
 31:
*32:      template <class ofType>
*33:          anAccumulator<ofType>::anAccumulator(void):
*34:              myValue(0)
*35:      {
*36:      };
 37:
 38:      template <class ofType>
 39:          anAccumulator<ofType>::anAccumulator
 40:              (anAccumulator &theAccumulator):
 41:                  myValue(theAccumulator.myValue)
 42:      {
 43:      };
 44:
*45:      template <class ofType>
*46:          anAccumulator<ofType>::~anAccumulator(void)
*47:      {
*48:      };
 49:
 50: };
 51:
 52: #endif
```

ANALYSIS Line 4 is the normal #include of aRequest.

Line 8 identifies the class as a template and the type parameter name as ofType.

Lines 32–34 are the constructor. You can see that template <class ofType> and anAccumulator<ofType> must be present, even though this constructor does not make use of the type parameter. If these are not present, the compiler will not know that this is a member function of the template class anAccumulator<ofType>.

The same is true for all the functions, including the virtual destructor implemented on lines 45–48.

Listing 25.5 shows aBasicAccumulator, now also a template.

LISTING 25.5   aBasicAccumulator **Template Header File**

```
1: #ifndef BasicAccumulatorModuleH
2: #define BasicAccumulatorModuleH
```

LISTING 25.5   Continued

```
 3:
*4: #include <string>
*5: #include <exception>
 6:
 7: #include "AccumulatorModule.h"
 8: #include "InstanceCountableModule.h"
 9:
10: namespace SAMSCalculator
11: {
*12:        template <class ofType> class aBasicAccumulator:
*13:            public anAccumulator<ofType>,
*14:            public isInstanceCountable
15:        {
16:            public:
17:
18:                aBasicAccumulator(void);
19:
20:                aBasicAccumulator
21:                    (aBasicAccumulator &theAccumulator);
22:
*23:                ofType Apply(const aRequest<ofType> &theRequest);
24:                ofType Value(void) const;
25:
*26:                anAccumulator<ofType>
*27:                    &ReferenceToANewAccumulator(void);
28:        };
29:
30:        using namespace std;
31:
32:        template <class ofType>
33:            aBasicAccumulator<ofType>::aBasicAccumulator(void)
34:        {
35:        };
36:
37:        template <class ofType>
38:            aBasicAccumulator<ofType>::aBasicAccumulator
39:                (aBasicAccumulator<ofType> &theAccumulator):
40:                    anAccumulator(theAccumulator)
41:        {
42:        };
43:
*44:        template <class ofType>
*45:            ofType aBasicAccumulator<ofType>::Apply
*46:                (const aRequest<ofType> &theRequest)
```

LISTING 25.5 Continued

```
47:    {
48:        switch (theRequest.Operator())
49:        {
50:           case add:
51:               myValue+= theRequest.Operand();
52:               break;
53:
54:           case subtract:
55:               myValue-= theRequest.Operand();
56:               break;
57:
58:           case multiply:
59:               myValue*= theRequest.Operand();
60:               break;
61:
62:           case divide:
63:               myValue/= theRequest.Operand();
64:               break;
65:
66:           default:
67:
68:               throw
69:                   runtime_error
70:                   (
71:                       string("SAMSCalculator::") +
72:                       string("aBasicAccumulator<ofType>::") +
73:                       string("Apply") +
74:                       string(" - Unknown operator.")
75:                   );
76:        };
77:
78:        return Value();
79:    };
80:
81:    template <class ofType>
82:        ofType aBasicAccumulator<ofType>::Value(void) const
83:    {
84:        return myValue;
85:    };
86:
*87:    template <class ofType>
*88:        anAccumulator<ofType>
*89:            &aBasicAccumulator<ofType>::
```

LISTING 25.5   Continued

```
*90:                ReferenceToANewAccumulator(void)
*91:    {
*92:        return *(new aBasicAccumulator<ofType>);
*93:    };
*94: };
 95:
 96: #endif
```

ANALYSIS   Lines 4 and 5 include headers needed by the implementation. As mentioned earlier, everything needed for the implementation must be present in the header file for the template to work.

Lines 12–14 show how aBasicAccumulator inherits from the template class anAccumulator and the non-template class isInstanceCountable. You can see on line 13 that the mention of the class anAccumulator also includes the angle brackets and the type parameter used for this class. This specialization makes sure anAccumulator has the correct type parameter to match aBasicAccumulator and that myValue will therefore be of the correct type. Line 14 shows that non-template classes are inherited normally and are not affected by the type parameter.

Line 23 is a function affected by the type parameter; of special note is the need to use the type parameter to specialize aRequest for the function argument theRequest. Specialization ensures that the operand of the request will be of the same type as anAccumulator::myValue because both will be of the type provided as the type parameter to aBasicAccumulator.

Lines 26 and 27 declare the function ReferenceToANewAccumulator(). In this case, the return type anAccumulator<ofType> has been specialized with the type parameter. This ensures that the new instance will be of the same class as the object from which the new instance was requested.

Lines 44–46 show the header for the Apply() function, which, on line 46, specializes aRequest to match the type parameter for this class. The rest of the function is essentially unchanged, except for the consequences of moving the enum for anOperator out of the aRequest class declaration on the values used in the cases of the switch statement (they are no longer prefixed by aRequest::).

Lines 87–95 show the new `ReferenceToNewAccumulator()`. Line 92 is the most interesting because it uses `new` to create an instance of the class `aBasicAccumulator<ofType>` and returns a reference to that instance as a reference to `anAccumulator<ofType>`. This demonstrates that class polymorphism works with template classes just as with non-template classes.

Using the Templates

Listing 25.6 shows how the `aRequest` and `aBasicAccumulator` templates are used by a new `main()` that acts as a test harness for these classes. This test harness instantiates two separate accumulators—one specialized for `float` and one specialized for `int`. As you might remember from Lesson 4, "Numeric Input," the integer calculator drops the fractional parts of numbers. When tested with `+3-2*3/2`, the `int` calculator produces `1` and the `float` calculator produces `1.5`.

LISTING 25.6 `main()` Using the Template Classes to Instantiate a `float` and `int` Calculator Test

```
 1: #include <iostream>
 2:
 3: #include "BasicAccumulatorModule.h"
 4: #include "RequestModule.h"
 5:
 6: using namespace std;
 7: using namespace SAMSCalculator;
 8:
 9: int main(int argc, char* argv[])
10: {
*11:     aBasicAccumulator<float>   Accumulator;
12:
*13:     Accumulator.Apply(aRequest<float>(add,3));
*14:     Accumulator.Apply(aRequest<float>(subtract,2));
*15:     Accumulator.Apply(aRequest<float>(multiply,3));
*16:     Accumulator.Apply(aRequest<float>(divide,2));
17:
18:     cout << "Result = " << Accumulator.Value() << endl;
19:
20:     char StopCharacter;
21:     cin >> StopCharacter;
22:
*23:     aBasicAccumulator<int>   IntAccumulator;
```

LISTING 25.6   Continued

```
24:
*25:        IntAccumulator.Apply(aRequest<int>(add,3));
*26:        IntAccumulator.Apply(aRequest<int>(subtract,2));
*27:        IntAccumulator.Apply(aRequest<int>(multiply,3));
*28:        IntAccumulator.Apply(aRequest<int>(divide,2));
29:
30:        cout << "Result = " << IntAccumulator.Value() << endl;
31:
32:        cin >> StopCharacter;
33:
34:        return 0;
35: }
```

ANALYSIS Line 11 declares aBasicAccumulator<float> Accumulator, specialized to use a float as the type parameter.

Lines 13–16 test this accumulator with a set of aRequest objects specialized as float. If aRequest<int> were used for the arguments instead of aRequest<float>, lines 13–16 would produce compiler error messages such as these:

```
[C++ Error] Main.cpp(13):
E2064 Cannot initialize 'const aRequest<float> &'
with 'aRequest<int>'
[C++ Error] Main.cpp(13):
E2342 Type mismatch in parameter 'theRequest'
(wanted 'const aRequest<float> &', got 'aRequest<int>')
```

Lines 13–16 instantiate aRequest<float> objects as the arguments to Accumulator.Apply(), making them effectively constants, unlike Accumulator, which is instantiated as a variable. Either way works for instantiating template classes, just as for any other classes.

Lines 23 and 25–28 run the same test for aBasicAccumulator and aRequest specialized as int.

Running the Test

When the test harness is run, this is the output it produces:

OUTPUT   Result = 1.5

INPUT   ·

OUTPUT   `Result = 1`

You can see that the `int` form of the accumulator has the problem with integer division demonstrated in Lesson 4. But it works as well as it can and demonstrates that `aBasicAccumulator` has, in fact, been instantiated for `int`.

A Few Notes on Templates

Here are a few additional facts about templates:

- Templates can have more than one type parameter. Type parameters are separated by commas. For instance:

  ```
  template <class ofOperandType, class ofOperatorType>
  class Something...
  ```

- Templates can inherit from other templates, non-template classes, or any combination of the two.

- Non-template classes can inherit from one or more templates specialized with appropriate type parameters, as in

  ```
  class aNonTemplateClass: public aTemplate<float>
  ```

More Strengths and Weaknesses

You can see from this lesson that templates offer some benefits. For instance, you've seen two different accumulators created without reimplementing the core classes—all that you have to do to change the data type of the accumulator is to change the value of the type parameter. The same benefits can be extended throughout the calculator by making the rest of the calculator classes into templates.

Templates work well with the strong typing that allows the C++ compiler to warn you about mistakes you have made in your code. The use of the type parameter in templates means that templates can work together in inheritance and in arguments to member functions and you can be sure that the fundamental data types used will agree. The compiler reminds you when types don't agree through error messages, so you can be sure that your program is correct in its use of types and type parameters when it compiles successfully.

> **Templates Have Risks** The entire implementation of a template is exposed in the header file. This makes it impossible to resell templates as third-party libraries without source code, or to be sure that callers are not relying on implementation details.
>
> The declaration of a template and its implementation use a fairly complex syntax. To make matters worse, many template authors use T rather than something more meaningful for the type parameter name—making the resulting code even more cryptic.
>
> Finally, some advanced C++ programmers use templates in complicated ways that can be very difficult for anyone to follow. Entire books can and have been written on templates because of this. Keep your use of templates simple.

Summing Up

In this lesson, you have seen template classes declared, defined, and instantiated. You have seen template classes used for arguments to member functions of other template classes and have seen how to use the type parameter to make sure that inherited and argument template classes are specialized to match the class that uses them, thus preserving C++ type safety. And, hopefully, you have learned the advantages and risks of using templates.

LESSON 26

Performance: C++ Optimizations

This lesson discusses ways to make your code perform better.

Running Faster, Getting Smaller

Every program can be made to run faster or to use less memory.

Many programmers claim to be able to predict what makes a program fast or slow, big or small. However, experience shows that programmers are not usually good at guessing in advance which parts of their programs will cause performance problems. And often, by trying to optimize a program prematurely, a programmer will not only create a slower, larger program, but will also make it unreadable and unmaintainable.

The best course is to create a well-structured program and then use tests to find what's slow or big. This enables you to focus on the features of C++ while programming and thus build a program that is less likely to need dramatic optimization.

Keep in mind that most performance optimization consists of trade-offs. You can increase the speed at which a program runs, but you may have to make it bigger or use more memory to accomplish this.

Inlining

C++ offers an easy way to gain speed at the cost of space.

A sophisticated object-oriented program may make millions of function calls per second. Even if each function call takes a tiny amount of time, reducing the overhead from such calls can sometimes make the difference between acceptable and unacceptable performance.

If testing indicates that reducing function calls can help performance (and it is usually only a tiny minority of calls that are repeated often enough to be usefully optimized), then *inlining* lets you eliminate function call overhead at the price of increased program size.

There are two ways to inline. The simplest is to put the function implementation in the class declaration, as in this (non-template) version of anAccumulator:

```
 1:      class aAccumulator
 2:      {
 3:          public:
 4:
 5:              anAccumulator(void);
 6:              anAccumulator(anAccumulator&theAccumulator);
 7:
 8:              virtual float Apply
                    ➥(const aRequest &theRequest) = 0;
 9:
*10:              float Value(void) const
*11:              {
*12:                  return myValue;
*13:              };
14:
15:              virtual anAccumulator
                    ➥&ReferenceToANewAccumulator(void) = 0;
16:
17:          protected:
18:
19:              float myValue;
20:      };
```

ANALYSIS   Lines 10–13 inline a getter function. Getters and setters are often good candidates for inlining because they are small and are called frequently.

As a result of this change, the program will insert the code that gets the content of myValue everywhere that Value() is called, rather than generating code to push space on the stack, call the function, get the result from the stack, and pop the result from the stack. Keep in mind, however, that modern computers and compilers are designed to make function calls and stack management very fast, so this may not buy you much performance improvement.

You can inline virtual functions as well as non-virtual functions, but the chances are that the compiler will ignore your request and create a normal function call. It will only inline a virtual function when it is absolutely sure that it knows the actual class of the instance the function is being called on.

Even non-virtual functions may or may not be inlined at the discretion of the compiler. For instance, a function that calls itself will not be inlined.

You can also inline in the implementation file when you don't want to reveal your member function's implementation. Simply use the `inline` keyword in the implementation file function head as follows:

```
inline float anAccumulator::Value(void) const
{
    return myValue;
};
```

Again, keep in mind that the compiler tries to ensure that your program behaves correctly, and it will ignore the `inline` keyword in some situations if it seems that inlining might cause a problem.

Incrementing and Decrementing

Almost every modern processor can increment and decrement in one machine instruction (and many can do it in a fraction of an instruction). Use of the ++ and - - operators enables C++ compilers to use special increment and decrement instructions in the code they generate from your C++ source. So by using

```
Index++;
```

rather than

```
Index = Index + 1;
```

you can help the compiler and speed up your program.

It is also possible that the compiler can optimize

```
Index+= 3;
```

to run faster than

```
Index = Index + 3;
```

for similar reasons.

Note that this will not help with overloaded operators, however, because they have user-defined implementations.

Templates Versus Generic Classes

Templates generate code in your program each time they are instantiated, so they make the program larger than generic classes. However, generic classes (which leverage class polymorphism) have to use virtual functions, which makes each function call slightly slower.

In any event, you should not let performance drive your decision between templates and class polymorphism unless the problems are severe and you can determine through performance measurements that they are the result of using or not using templates.

Timing Your Code

You should always time your code to find out which parts of it are slow. This is an excellent application for test harnesses.

The Standard C library provides a `time` function for you to use. Unfortunately, it only measures time in one-second increments, so you will have to run many tests to get a time you can measure. For instance:

```
#include <time.h>

time_t Start;
time_t End;

time(&Start);
```

```
for (int Index = 0; Index < 100000; Index++)
{
    int Value = Accumulator.Value();
};

time(&end);

double TimeRequired = difftime(Start,End);
```

Keep in mind that some operations cannot be easily or reliably performed in a loop of this sort. For instance:

```
#include <time.h>

time_t Start;
time_t End;

time(&Start);

for (int Index = 0; Index < 100000; Index++)
{
    int Value = Accumulator.Apply(aRequest(aRequest::add,34));
};

time(&end);

double TimeRequired = difftime(Start,End);
```

This code applies 100,000 requests to the accumulator, which means that you might actually be testing the effects of a large tape rather than the speed of the calculation. Make sure that you carefully consider what you are testing.

In any event, properly gathered timings are the only way to pinpoint which parts of your program need optimization.

You can use timing test harnesses to find out whether your changes have actually succeeded in speeding up your program.

Also, don't forget that you can use a profiler to see where your program spends its time, as discussed in Lesson 23, "Object Testing Using Inheritance."

Program/Data Structure Size

A program's size can affect the time it takes for it to start. In addition, a larger program or a program with large data structures can take up enough memory to force the operating system to keep moving pieces of the program back and forth from disk, which drastically hinders performance.

Unfortunately, size can be very difficult to control. Most modern object-oriented programs depend on a vast and complex set of in-house and vendor-supplied libraries to perform all the functions users demand and to provide the graphical user interfaces most programs need. You can only rarely do without these libraries and can almost never reduce their size. The best you can hope for is a compiler optimization flag that causes the compiler to drop any code you never call.

In-memory data structures are often used to improve speed. Sometimes you can reduce their size by deleting heap-allocated structures as soon as they are not needed, or by using stack rather than heap allocation.

It can be helpful to measure how your program uses memory over time. Look for large objects that hang around for the life of your program even though they are needed only briefly.

Summing Up

Performance optimization can only be performed starting with a well-crafted and maintainable object-oriented program. Given that, you should perform careful timings to make sure you've isolated the actual source of the performance problem. Once you have a target, C++ offers some language features that may help.

Once you have made changes, you need to rerun your tests to determine whether they have had any effect.

However, keep in mind that many performance problems result from problems with your program logic or from overhead accessing files or databases. There are numerous texts on algorithms that discuss the relative speeds of alternate approaches to specific programming challenges and you should make sure to consult those as well when optimizing your programs.

Finally, keep in mind that the size of data structures and the size of generated program code can affect performance. You may have to give up some speed to create a smaller program.

LESSON 27
Wrapping Up

This lesson summarizes the key points that you have learned and suggests ways in which you can further improve the calculator.

Things You Can Do to Enhance the Calculator

You have worked on the calculator throughout this book, transforming it again and again, either to add capabilities or to reorganize it and make it easier to understand.

Now you can carry on that work and add some capabilities yourself.

Add Undo/Redo Capabilities

You can undo the effects of calculations by setting the accumulator to zero and replaying the tape to the request before the last one on the tape. You can even keep two extra tapes—an undo tape that contains all the requests that haven't been undone, and a redo tape that contains requests that have been undone. Then an undo operator can swap the last entry from the undo tape to the redo tape, clear the accumulator, and replay the undo tape.

Add Named Variables

The Standard C++ library offers a container called map that can be used to store named values. A calculator that lets you input a value with a name and then use it in a calculation would be much more powerful than the existing calculator.

Use in a More Powerful Program Such as a Spreadsheet

You can also create a text-oriented spreadsheet-like program using the calculator to generate the results for each cell. In fact, you could instantiate a separate calculator for each cell of the spreadsheet to make things easier. You could use static variables in your classes to share information between cells.

Use with a Graphical User Interface

You can add a windowed user interface to your calculator or spreadsheet. The objects you've created here are largely independent of the external interface, which means that it's easy to replace a character-based user interface with one for Windows, Unix, or Macintosh.

Lessons Learned

You've taken a program from a few short lines to a fully object-oriented collection of several classes in many files.

If you are a professional programmer, you should now realize how well C++ supports every aspect of program development.

And if you've never programmed before, you've had the opportunity to go through several complete development and maintenance cycles, experiencing all the activities that are part of the life of the professional programmer.

Thinking in Terms of Classes and Objects

You can envision a program as a list of instructions, a set of functions, or a set of classes and objects. Of these viewpoints, seeing a program as classes and objects offers the greatest opportunity to structure programs in a way that reflects how you think.

The following features of C++ support classes and objects:

- Class declarations and definitions
- Instance creation on the stack

- Instance creation and deletion using the heap

- Virtual functions and class polymorphism

- Function and operator overloading

- Templates

Evolving a Program

In the course of creating this program, you've seen that C++ supports both procedural and object-oriented programming, and that it offers features to help you smoothly grow a simple program into a complex one.

C++ is an excellent language for evolving programs as a result of the many types and levels of abstraction it provides. You've learned about

- Functional abstraction

- Data abstraction

- Modules

- Classes and objects with member functions and variables

- Inheritance and class polymorphism

- Templates

Refactoring Frequently

Always remember that refactoring a program into new configurations of these abstractions is a critical responsibility of the programmer. Through careful refactoring as complexity increases, you can make a program clearer and easier to understand over time. Without it, the ever-increasing maintenance demands will gradually reduce the program into chaos.

Maintaining the Contract

Object-oriented programming works because objects present a specific interface that makes a contract with any user of the object. You have refactored and reimplemented this program and its objects many times, and each time you have made sure that objects and functions retain this expected behavior.

C++ offers many features that help maintain the contract:

- Strong typing enforced by the compiler
- Requirement to declare types, constants, and variables before they can be used
- Inheritance and class polymorphism
- Abstract classes (interfaces)
- Multiple inheritance
- Templates

Testing Frequently

Changes require testing, and you've made a lot of changes and performed a lot of testing. Now you know that C++ makes it easy to create many kinds of test harnesses and you know how to test at every level of abstraction. Objects can test themselves or each other, or can even be combined into partial systems for the purpose of incrementally testing additions or changes.

Thinking About Performance at the Right Time

Hopefully, this book has encouraged you to think about the best way to organize programs using the features of the C++ language. Once you have built a program that is structurally sound, it is much easier to improve its performance by optimizing specific objects based on testing and timing.

Doing Things Simply

C++ is a highly developed language with a wide variety of features, many of which you have seen, but some of which have been treated lightly or not at all for the sake of simplicity. There is a best way to use each language feature for maximum clarity.

You have continually refactored and redeveloped the calculator to make it simpler and easier to understand. This effort has always paid off by lowering the risk of introducing new errors during maintenance.

Naming Things Well

A program works just as well when you name things poorly as when you name things in a clear and understandable fashion. But naming things carefully makes it easier to understand what you are doing wrong, or what an unfamiliar section of a program means.

In this book, you have seen a naming convention that focuses on the type, source, scope, and lifetime of things in addition to their meaning in the context of the program. This naming convention is only one of many that you can use, and if you use class libraries from other programmers, you will have to learn and adapt to many naming conventions, perhaps even dealing with several at the same time. Hopefully, you will remain focused on naming, applying as much attention to that as to program structure and purpose.

Being Patient with the Compiler and Yourself

Now you know a little bit about thinking like a compiler. This will help when you get a confusing error message, or when something that seems perfectly correct won't compile. Being patient with yourself will help you when the program won't run or continually produces errors. And eventually, you will have all the techniques you need to regularly produce programs that are low in errors and high in reliability.

No program is perfect, so any program can be improved. As you understand more about the C++ language and about programming, you will change and adapt your programs to reflect your increased knowledge.

Be patient—all it takes is time, experience, and thought.

APPENDEX A
Operators

The table in this appendix lists and describes the many operators of the C++ language. Many of these operators are available for overloading in your classes.

When overloading the operators, you are not restricted to the types indicated here. Often the type will be your class. You can also overload any infix operator more than once to work with different types, but remember that the return type is not part of what differentiates two overloads.

Arithmetic Operators

Operator	Name/Meaning	Works On	Overload	Example	Reads As
+	Add	Numeric and char	Y	a+b	Add a and b to produce a result
-	Subtract	Numeric and char	Y	a - b	Subtract b from a to produce a result
*	Multiply	Numeric and char	Y	a*b	Multiply a by b to produce a result
/	Divide	Numeric and char	Y	a/b	Divide a by b to produce a result
++	Increment or decrement	Numeric and char	Y	a++ ++a	Provide a as a result and then add 1 to a, or add 1 to a and provide that as a result
--				a - - - - a	Provide a as a result and then subtract 1 from a, or subtract 1 from a and provide that as a result
%	Modulo	Numeric and char	Y	a%b	Provide the remainder from dividing a by b

Assignment Operators

=	Assign	Any	Y	a=b	Make the contents of a the same as the contents of b
+= -= *= /=	Arithmetic assignment operators	Numeric and char	Y	a+=b	Equivalent to a = a + b Make the contents the same as they would be if the right-hand side were a+b

Relational/Logical Operators

!	Negation	Bool	Y	!a	If a is true, make it false; if a is false, make it true
==	Equal	Any	Y	a == b	If the contents of a are equal to the contents of b, this expression is true; otherwise, it is false
!=	Not equal	Any	Y	a != b	If the contents of a are not equal to the contents of b, this expression is true; otherwise, it is false
>	Greater than	Any	Y	a > b	If the contents of a are greater than the contents of b, this expression is true; otherwise, it is false

Relational/Logical Operators (continued)

Operator	Name/Meaning	Works On	Overload	Example	Reads As
<	Less than	Any	Y	a < b	If the contents of a are less than the contents of b, this expression is true; otherwise, it is false
>=	Greater than or equal	Any	Y	a >= b	If the contents of a are greater than or less than b, this expression is true; otherwise, it is false
<=	Less than or equal	Any	Y	a <= b	If the contents of a are less than or equal to the contents of b, this expression is true; otherwise, it is false
&&	And	Bool	Y	a && b	if a is true and b is true, this expression is true; otherwise, it is false
||	Or	Bool	Y	a || b	if a is true or b is true, this expression is true; otherwise, it is false

Bitwise Operators[1]

&	And	Y	Integer numeric, char, or bool	a & b	Produce a number with bits set to 1 where the bits in a and b are the same
		Or	Y	Integer numeric, char, or bool	a | b	Produce a number with bits set to 1 where the bits in a or b are 1
^	XOr (exclusive Or)	Y	Integer numeric, char, or bool	a ^ b	Produce a number with bits set to 1 where the bits in a and b have the same value and set to 0 where they are different
<<	Left shift	Y	Integer numeric, char, or bool	a<<b	Produce a number whose bits are those of a shifted left by the number of bits represented by b
>>	Right shift	Y	Integer numeric, char, or bool	a>>b	Produce a number whose bits are those of a shifted right by the number of bits represented by b
~	One's complement or "bit negation"	Y	Integer numeric, char, or bool	~a	Produce a number whose bits are 0 where they were 1 and vice versa

Operator	Name/Meaning	Works On	Overload	Example	Reads As
Bitwise Operators (continued)					
&= |= ^= ~= >>= <<=	Bitwise assignment operators	Integer numeric, char, or bool	Y	a&= b	Produce a number whose bits are a and b and assign to a
Pointer Operations[2]					
&	Address of	Any	Y (not recommended)	&a	Produce the number that is the location of the content of a
*	Dereference	Any	Y (not recommended)	*a	Produce the content at the location pointed to by the content of a
++ - -	Increment and decrement	Pointer	Y (see arithmetic increment and decrement)	a++	Increment the pointer a to point to the next addressable location

Reference Operator

&	Address of	Any	Y (not recommended)	&a	Produce the number that is the location of the content referred to by a

Cast Operators[3]

static_ cast	Static cast	Any	N, but will use traditional cast override (see below)	static_ cast <type>(a)	Convert a to *type* if type rules allow or if there is a traditional cast override
cast	Cast (traditional)	Any	Y	(*type*)a	Convert a to *type* whether or not type rules allow

Cast Operators (continued)

Operator	Name/Meaning	Works On	Overload	Example	Reads As
dynamic_cast	Dynamic cast or class cast	Any class pointer or reference	N	dynamic_cast <anOther Class*>(&a) or dynamic_cast <anOther Class &>(a)	View this class pointer or reference as a pointer or reference to its indicated superclass or derived class
const_cast	Const cast	Any variable	N	const_cast<type> (a)	View this class or pointer as const or non-const based on the cast
reinter-pret_cast	Reinterpret cast	Any variable	N	reinter-pret_cast <type>a	View this variable as type, whether or not the type system allows it; this is the same as a traditional cast

Conditional Operator

?:	If expression	Any	N	a ? b : c	If a is true, produce the value of b; otherwise, produce the value of c

Storage Operators

new	Operator new	Type	Y	new *type*	Produce a pointer to an area of storage large enough for *type*
delete	Delete	Any pointer	Y	delete a delete [] a	Release the storage for variable a or array a back to the heap

Scope Operator

::	Scope resolution	Names	N	*namespace* ::*name* *namespace* ::*class* ::*name* *class*:: *nested* *class*:: *name*	Resolve the name by specifying the context where it can be found by the compiler

Operator	Name/Meaning	Works On	Overload	Example	Reads As
Member Access Operators					
.	Dot operator selection or member	Structured or class type and member	N	`object` `.member`	Provide the content of or call the member of the object
->	Arrow operator or pointer member selection operator	Structured or class type pointer and member	N	`object` `pointer` `->member` `name`	Dereference the object pointer and provide the content of or call the member of the object
Pointer to Member Operators					
.*	Pointer to member	Class object and pointer to member	N	`a.*b`	Get the content of the member of a whose slot is pointed to by b
->*	Pointer to member	Class pointer and pointer to member of class	N	`a->*b`	Get the content of the member of *a whose slot is pointed to by b

Miscellaneous Operators

( )	Function call operator	Function name or object with overload	Y	*name* ( )	Call the function, which may be an overload in the class
[ ]	Subscript operator	Array or object with overload	Y	*name* [ ]	Get the array element or call the overload in the object

1 *Bitwise operators work on individual bits of a simple type; there are typically 8 bits per* char, *16 bits per* short int, *32 bits per* int, *and so on. Bitwise operators consider operands to be base two (binary) numbers, regardless of their actual type.*

2 *All arithmetic operations can be performed on a pointer. The compiler does not prevent the result from pointing to an invalid location.*

3 *Cast operators convert one type to another—see* http://anubis.dkuug.dk/JTC1/SC22/WG21/docs/papers/1993/N0349a.pdf *for more information from the designer of C++.*

APPENDIX B

Operator Precedence

It is important to understand that operators have a precedence, but it is not essential to memorize the precedence.

Precedence is the order in which a program performs the operations in a formula. If one operator has precedence over another operator, it is evaluated first.

Higher precedence operators "bind tighter" than lower precedence operators; thus, higher precedence operators are evaluated first. Table B.1 lists the C++ operators by precedence.

TABLE B.1 Operator Precedence

Rank	Name	Operator
1	Scope resolution	::
2	Member selection, subscripting,	. ->
	function calls, postfix increment	( )
	and decrement	++ --
3	Prefix increment and decrement,	++ --
	complement, and, not, unary minus and plus,	^ !
	address of and dereference, new, new[], delete,	- +
	delete[], casting, size of, sizeof()	& *
		( )
4	Member selection for pointer	.* ->*
5	Multiply, divide, modulo	* / %
6	Add, subtract	+ -

Rank	Name	Operator
7	Shift	`<< >>`
8	Inequality relational	`< <= > >=`
9	Equality, inequality	`== !=`
10	Bitwise and	`&`
11	Bitwise exclusive or	`^`
12	Bitwise or	`|`
13	Logical and	`&&`
14	Logical or	`||`
15	Conditional	`?:`
16	Assignment operators	`= *= /= %=`
		`+= -= <<= >>=`
		`&= |= ^=`
17	Throw operator	`throw`
18	Comma	`,`

INDEX

SYMBOLS

! operator, 38, 74
&, 105
*, 98-99, 104
++ operator, 92, 265
-- operator, 92
|| operator, 74
-> (pointer member selection), 127
<< operator, 18
>> operator, 24
&& relational operator, 117
\ (backslash), 23
// (double-slash comment), 17
(pound symbol), 15
:: (scope resolution operator), 64
/* (slash-star comment), 17
- symbol, 158

A

a prefix, 123
aBasicAccumulator, 236
    modifying, 254
abstract classes, 230-233
accessing member variables, 167
Accumulate function, 83-84, 93-94
Accumulator(), using enumerations
    in, 123-125
accumulators, 109
actual arguments, 48
adding
    instance counts to classes, 238
    member functions, 206
    operands, 109
    redo capabilities, 270
    undo capabilities, 270
addition operators, 39
addresses, 130-132
aggregation, 238
allocating memory, 24
ambiguous overloads, 196
"an" (name prefix), 123
anAccumulator class, 229
    modifying, 254
ancestors, 206
and (&&) operator, 76

anExternalInterface class, 198, 230
    user interfaces, 184
argc, 144
argument count, 144
argument value, 140
arguments, 48
    actual, 48
    char* argv[ ], 11
    const char *, 70
    formal, 48, 52
    int argc, 11
    optional, 113
    theThingWeAreDoing, 70
argv, 140
arrays, 88
    creating, 88, 99
    defining, 88
    deleting, 107
    destroying, 99
    myOperand, 99
    myOperator, 99
    parallel, 90
    pointers, 99
    referencing, 92
    resizing, 96
    size, 90, 99
ASCII (American Standard Code for
    Information Interchange), 25
assigning addresses, 132
assignment operators, 26
    overloading, 203
associations, 157
aTape class, 229
attributes, 157

B

backslashes, 23
bang (!) operator, 38, 76
blank lines. *See* whitespace

blocks, 11
body, 11
    functions, 48
bool expressions, 37, 75-76
    Boole, George 38
    cin.fail( ), 38
    creating, 76
bool variables, 78
Boole, George, 38
Boolean algebra, 38
boundary value tests, 226
braces, 11
    whitespace, 17
breaks, 82
bugs, 10
bundling sets of variables, 126
bytes, 24

C

C++
    case sensitivity, 11, 28
    punctuation, 11
C++ features
    support for classes, 271
    support for objects, 271
calculating, 31
calculations, performing, 30
calculator tape, creating, 88-91
calculators, 30, 82
    testing, 109
callbacks, 143, 178
    creating, 133
calling
    class member functions, 148
    functions, 18, 46, 62-64, 230,
        243
    main( ) function, 17
    modules, 62, 64
    operator member functions, 199
    superclasses, 220
calls, resolving, 195

capacity tests, 225
case sensitivity, 11, 28
catch statements, 42
cerr statements, 39
changing
    control flow, 81
    internal state, 168
char, 23
    restrictions, 122
char* argv, 11
character sets, ASCII, 25
character variables, 27
characters
    end-of-line, 18
    pending, 39
    zeroth, 99
checking number of words on command line, 144
cin statements, 39, 44, 51
cin.fail(), 38
class declarations, 146-147, 156, 163
class definitions, 166
class diagrams, 157
    UML, 158
class functions, 243
class implementation, 166
class keyword, 146
class libraries
    freeware, 179
    shareware, 179
    Standard C++, 179
    using, 180
class member functions, calling, 148
class polymorphism, 213, 231, 235
class programmers, 237
class-level variable, 243
classes, 145
    abstract, 230
        creating, 231
        implementing, 233
    anAccumulator, 229
    and speed, 266
    anExternalInterface, 230
    aRequest, 166

aTape, 229
    concrete, 231
    declaring, 156
    versus instances, 145
    isInstanceCountable, 238
    persistent, 206
    private sections, 216
    protected sections, 216
    support for, 271
    testing, 224
    UML, 159, 161
classnames, specifying, 167
cleaning up code, 45
closing streams, 137-138
code
    cleaning up, 45
    compiler error demonstration, 12
    dropping, 268
    error-handling, 42
    exception-handling, 42
    generating, using templates, 248
    main.cpp, 14
    modifying, 15
    moving lines into functions, 53
    normal processing, 42
    refactoring, 54
    running, 37, 57, 66
        loops, 66
    separating units of code into functions, 53
    timing, 266
coding templates, 248
cohesion, functions, 53
comma operator, 118
commands
    compile, 64-65
    link, 65
comments, 17
    double-slash (//), 17
    slash-star (/*), 17
compile-time errors, 12-13, 79

compiler optimization flags, dropping code not called, 268
compiler-generated copy constructors, 181
compilers, 64
    compile-time errors, 12-13
    defined, 8
compiling
    commands, 64
    programs, 58
complex expressions, nesting parentheses, 22
components, iostream, 15
compound statements, 11
comprehensive test harness, 223
concrete classes, 231
    simulators, 237
    stubs, 237
condition, 91
console input/output, 7
const char * argument, 70
const keyword, 202
constants, 26
constructors, 150
    copy, 154, 181
    default, 151
    multiple, 152
    overloaded, 197
    private, 150
control flow, changing, 81
control structures, 67
controlling flow, 82
conventions, 52
    naming, 172, 274
copy constructors, 154
    compiler-generated, 181
copy statements, 104
coupling functions, 53
cout output stream, 31
cout statements, 15, 18, 22, 33
.cpp files, modules, 11

creating
    arrays, 88, 99
    bool expressions, 76
    calculator tape, 88-91
    callbacks, 133
    classes, abstract, 231
    derived tests, 226
    header files, 58-59
    interfaces, 229
    lists of structures, 128
    objects, 146
    programs, 11
    regression tests, 226
    reports, using profilers, 225
    structures, 127
    test harnesses, 223

D

data, retaining, 136
data locations, addresses, 130
datatypes, UML, 158
deallocated storage, 184
debuggers, IDE (Integrated Development Environment), 118
debugging
    programs, 35
    statements, 33
declarations
    class, 163
    namespaces, 61-62
declaring
    classes, 156
    function pointers, 131
    functions, 54-55
    inheritance, 206, 208
    member functions, 147
    member variable, 147
    structure types, 126
    templates, 248
    variables, 27, 149
    virtual destructors, 244

decreasing values, 92
decrement operators, 92
decrementing, 92
    instance counts, 243
    for performance optimization,
        265
default arguments, overloading, 195
default case, 82, 125
default constructors, 151
    preventing use of, 211
defensive programming, 31
#defines, 119
defining
    arrays, 88
    function body, 47
    function headers, 47
    functions, 47, 54
    variables, 24
delete keyword, 104
deleting
    arrays, 107
    heap-allocated structures, 127
    pointers, 106
dereferencing, 99
    operators, 104
    pointers, 127
designing
    functions, 46
    programs, 9
destroying arrays, 99
destructors, 153
developers
    Bjarne Stroustrup, 6
    Brian Kernighan, 6
    Dennis Ritchie, 6
development cycles, 9-10
diagrams
    class, 157
    object-oriented programs, draw-
        ing, 157
discovering errors, 118-119
discovering problems using cout
    statements, 33

displaying program results on screen,
    18
distinguishing overloaded functions,
    193-195
Divide function, 52
Dividend variable, 31, 40-41, 51
dividing by operands, 109
Divisor variable, 31, 40-41
do/while loops, 67
    running, 67
double-slash comment (//), 17
drawing diagrams of object-oriented
    programs, 157
dropping code, 268

E

editors, defined, 8
Element() member function, 211
elements, 88
    referencing, 88
    zeroth, 99
eliminating function call overhead,
    264
else keyword, 41
empty tests, 224
encapsulation, 86, 146
endl characters, 18
enhancing
    the calculator, 270-271
    programs, 53
enumerated types, 122
    syntax, 122
enumerations, in Accumulator(), 123,
    125
error
    messages, 39
    recovery, 39
error-handling code, 42
errors, 39, 42, 108
    compile, 79
    compile-time, 12-13
    discovering, 118

fatal, 71
handling, 45
heap allocation, 115
input, 40-41, 43-44
Main.cpp program, 16
punctuation, 12
recovering from, 36-37, 40-41
runtime, discovering, 119
evaluating
expressions, 21
precedence, operators, 233-234
exception handling, 42
input errors, 43-44
exceptions
iostream, 44
runtime_error, 84
throwing, 44-45, 81, 86
executing functions, 18
expressions, 20, 81
bool, 37
in cout statements, 22
evaluating, 21
nesting parentheses, 22
reading, 76
using parentheses, 21
extractor, 24

F

factory, 236
false values, 38
fatal errors, 71
files
.exe, 64
header, 57-58
implementation, 57-61
intermediate, 64
iostream.h, 16
.obj, 64
referencing, 137

float, 32
restrictions, 122
floating-point variables, 27
flow, controlling, 82
flow of control, 131
for keyword, 29
for loop, 91
condition, 91
initialization, 91
step, 91
formal arguments, 48, 52
freeware, 8
front-end test harness, 223
fstream, 136
function calls
optimizing, 264
signatures, 193
function headers, parts of, 47
function pointers, 131
assignment, 132
declaring, 131
functions, 11, 46, 49-51, 95
Accumulate, 83-84, 93-94
arguments, 48
body, 11, 48
braces, 11
calling, 18, 46, 62-64, 230, 243
class, 243
cohesion, 53
for converting operators, 189
coupling, 53
declaring, 54-55
defining, 47, 54
design, 46
Divide, 52
executing, 18
GetDividend, 52
getter, 165, 184
headers, 11, 48
defining, 47
identifying as members of a
class, 148

main(), 11, 46, 52
  calling, 17
  member, 145
    Apply(), 158
    Value(), 158
  moving lines of code into, 54
open(), 136
OtherFunction(), 216
overloaded, distinguishing, 193,
  195
overriding, 214
parameters, 48
precedence, 53
private, 58
prototypes, 59
  in the header, 87
public, 58
pure virtual, 230
returning
  values, 18
  void, 18
SelfTest(), 114, 175
setter, 184
SomeFunction(), 216
static, 243
StreamTape(), 138
Tape(), 99, 138
TestOK, 115
ThirdFunction(), 216
time, 266
UserWantsToContinue, 69, 73
validating, 116
virtual, initializing, 230

G-H

generating code using templates, 248
GetDividend function, 52
getter functions, 165
  services, 184

getting
  addresses, 131
  member variable values, 126
  numeric input, 40-41
global variables, 55
  issues, 55

handling errors, 45
header files, 57-58
  creating, 58-59
  iostream.h, 15
headers, 11
  functions, 48
heap, 97
heap allocation, errors, 115
heap-allocated structures, dereferencing, 127
heaps
  pointers, 98
  versus stacks, 95-97

I-J

IDE (Integrated Development
  Environment), 23, 118
identifying functions as members of
  a class, 148
if keyword, 29
if statements, 37, 81, 95
  else, 41
  format, 38
ifstream, 136
implementation, 230
  files, 57-61
implementing
  abstract classes, 233
  template classes, 248
improving speed in-memory data
  structures, 268
in-memory data structures, improving speed, 268
#include instruction, 16

increasing
    size of variables, 104
    values, 92
increment operators, 92
incrementing, 92
    instance counts, 243
    for performance optimization,
        265
indexes, 88
infix operators, 39
information hiding, 86, 146
inheritance
    ancestors, 206
    class polymorphism, 213
    declaring, 206, 208
    multiple, 238
    pattern of, 214
    restrictions, 211
    superclasses, 206
    trees, 214
        with abstract classes, 237
        with abstract classes and
            multiple inheritance, 239
inheriting from superclasses, 238
initialization, 91
initializers, 151
initializing, 31
    instances, 167
    member variables, 150-151
    programs, 51
    virtual functions, 230
inline keyword, 265
inlining, 264
    getter functions, 264
    in implementation files, 265
    non-virtual functions, 265
    virtual functions, 265
input errors, 40-44
inserters, 18
instance counts
    adding to classes, 238
    decrementing, 243
    incrementing, 243

instances
    versus classes, 145
    initializing, 167
instantiating objects, 146
    from a template, 249
instantiation, 146
int, 25, 31
    restrictions, 122
    returning, 18
int argc argument, 11
integer division, 31
integer variables, 27
integers
    signed, 27
    unsigned, 27
Integrated Development Environment
    (IDE), 23, 118
integrating classes, 231
integration, 231
integration programmers, 237
interfaces, 230
    creating, 229
    guidelines for programmers,
        230
intermediate files, 64
internal state, 168
iostream, 15, 22
    exceptions, 44
    header file, 15
    library, 15, 18, 44
iostream.h files, 16
is a
    differences from uses/has, 238
    relationships, 238
isInstanceCountable class, 238
ISO/ANSI, 1998 standard, 38
ISO/ANSI standard C++, 7

K-L

keywords, 29
    class, 146
    const, 202

delete, 104
else, 41
float, 32
for, 29
if, 29
inline, 265
int, 32
main, 29
new, 104
operator, 200
private, 147
public, 147
then, 41
this, 201
typedef, 132
virtual, 154, 217, 230
while, 29

languages
strongly typed, 6
weakly typed, 6
left-shift operator (>>), 197
libraries, 7
catching exceptions, 44
iostream, 15, 18, 44
namespaces, 16
throwing exceptions, 45
lines, replacing, 20
linked lists, 128
linkers, 57
linking structures, 128
literals, 18, 24
string, 18
local variables, static, 90
long int, 25
loops, 95
do/while, 67
for, 91
nesting, 73
refactoring, 73

stopping, 92
while, 69, 71-72

M-N

main
function, 11
keyword, 29
main() function, 46, 52, 240
calling, 17
returning, int, 18
main.cpp, 190, 212
program, 14
errors, 16
manual test harness, 223
member functions, 145
in abstract classes, calling, 231
adding, 206
declaring, 147
Element(), 211
NumberOfElements(), 211
replacing, 206
member selection (.) operator, 126, 134
member variable values
getting, 126
setting, 126
member variables
allocating from the heap, 154
declaring, 147
initializing, 150-151
private, indicating, 158
memory
allocating, 24
bytes, 24
leaks, 107
method polymorphism, 213
misusing operator overloads, 198

modifying
    aBasicAccumulator, 254
    anAccumulator, 254
    code, 15
modules, 11, 57
    calling, 62, 64
    compiling programs, 58
multiple
    constructors, 152
    inheritance, 238
multiplying by operands, 109
"my" (name prefix), 171

name clashes, avoiding, 165
named values, storing, 270
namespaces, 16, 61-62
    qualifiers, 16
    SAMSCalculator, 158
naming, 16
    classes, overloading, 192-193
    conventions, 172, 274
        formal arguments, 52
    standards, 171-172
    variables, 56
        avoiding keywords, 29
nested parentheses, 75
nesting
    loops, 73
    parentheses, 22
new
    keyword, 104
    operator, 97
normal processing code, 42
not operator, 38
NULL, 106
NumberOfElements( ) member
    function, 211
numeric input, 40-41
    getting, 36-37

O

.obj files, 64
object life span, 160
object-oriented
    patterns, 236
    programming, 6
objects, 145
    creating, 146
    instantiating, 146
    ownership of, 178
    support for, 271
    user interface, 184
ofstream, 136
OO patterns, 236
open() function, 136
opening streams, 138
operands
    adding, 109
    subtracting, 109
operator, 24
    keyword, 200
    member functions
        calling, 199
        overloading, 200
operator polymorphism, 213
operators, 109
    !, 38, 74-76
    ++, 92, 265
    --, 92, 265
    ||, 74-76
    >>, overloading, 198
    -> (pointer member selection),
        127
    addition, 39
    and (&&), 76
    bang, 38, 74-76
    comma, 118
    infix, 39
        *creating complex bool
        expressions, 76*

left-shift, 197
member selection (.), 126, 134
new, 97
not, 38, 74-76
or (||), 74-76
overloading, 197, 201
  misuse, 198
postfix, 92-93
precedence, 21, 233
  evaluating, 233-234
prefix, 92-93
prefix unary, 39
relational, 75
  &&, 117
scope resolution, 64, 148
optimization, testing for, 263
optimizing
  function calls, 264
  performance, 263
optional arguments, 113
or (||) operator, 76
organizing programs, 273
our prefix, 243
out-of-bounds tests, 33, 224
output
  standard, 8
  streams, cout, 31
overload resolution, 195
overloaded
  constructors, 197
  functions, distinguishing,
    193-195
overloading, 192-193, 209
  >> operator, 198
  assignment operators, 203
  default arguments, 195
  operator member functions, 200
  operators, 197, 201
  relational operators, 197
overloads, ambiguous, 196

overriding, 209
  functions, 214
  virtual keyword, 217
  superclass members, 211
ownership of objects, 178

P-Q

parallel arrays, 90
parameters, 48. See also arguments
parentheses, 76
  nested, 75
  nesting, 22
  using, 21
parts of programs, 11
pattern of inheritance (inheritance
  tree), 214
pending characters, 39
performance
  optimizing, 263
  tests, 225
performing calculations, 30
planning programming, 7
pointer member selection operator,
  127
pointers, 98-99
  arrays, 99
  dangers of, 105
  deleting, 106
  dereferencing, 127
  redirecting, 104
polymorphism
  class, 213
  method, 213
  operator, 213
popped space, 96
popping, 95
postfix operators, 92-93
pound symbol (#), 15

precedence, 53, 233
    operators, 21, 233
        evaluating, 233-234
prefix operators, 92-93
prefix unary operator, 39
prefixes, 123, 153
    argument, 171
    my, 86, 171
    our, 243
    the, 86
    type, 171
preprocessors
    include instruction, 16
    pound symbol (#), modifying
        code, 15
private
    constructor, 150
    functions, 58
    keywords, 147
    member variables, 158
    members, 147, 165
    sections, accessing member
        variables, 167
problems, discovering using cout
    statements, 33
procedural programming, 6
profilers, 225, 267
    creating reports, 225
programmers
    class, 237
    integration, 237
programming
    defensive, 31
    development cycles, 9
    gaining speed, 263
    object-oriented, 6
    organization, 121
    planning, 7
    preparing for, 7
    procedural, 6
    punctuation errors, 12
    reorganization, 121

styles, object-oriented, 6
    using classes, 179
programs
    calling functions, 18
    classes, 157
    compiling, 58
    creating, 11
    debugging, 35
    designing, 9
    displaying results on screen, 18
    enhancing, 53
    evolving, 272
    implementing, 27
    initializing, 51
    main.cpp, 14
    organizing, 273
    parts of, 11
    refactoring, 53
    repairing, 53
    restoring, 115
    stopping, 71
    testing, 56
prompts, 24
prototypes, 55, 59
public
    functions, 58
    keyword, 147
    member variables, 170
    members, 147, 165
punctuation, 11
    errors, 12
pure virtual functions, 230
pushed, 95

R

reading expressions, 76
recalling the tape, 141
reconstructing the calculator as an
    object-oriented program, 161
recovering from errors, 36-37, 39

redirecting pointers, 104
redo, 270
refactoring, 53, 272
    code, 54
    loops, 73
    programs, 53
references, 105, 135
ReferenceToANewAccumulator, 236
referencing
    arrays, 92
    elements, 88
    files, 137
regression testing, 32, 65
regression tests
    creating, 226
    running, 226
relational operators, 75
    equal to, 75
    greater than, 75
    greater than or equal to, 75
    less than, 75
    less than or equal to, 75
    not equal to, 75
    overloading, 197
relationships
    between instances
        has, 238
        uses, 238
        is a, 238
replacing
    lines, 20
    member functions, 206
reserving space, 97
resizing arrays, 96
resolving calls, 195
restoring programs, 115
retaining data, 136
return value, 12
ReturnCode variable, 39
returning functions
    values, 18
    void, 18

risks of templates, 262
running
    code, 37, 66
    regression tests, 226
    self-tests, 117
    tests, 260
runtime_error exceptions, 84
runtime errors, 119

S

saving, 138
scope, 137
scope resolution operator (::), 64, 148
self-testing, 111
self-tests
    discovering errors, 118
    running, 117
SelfTest() function, 114, 175
separately compiled files.
    See modules
separating code into related
    statements, 17
setter function, services, 184
setting member variable values, 126
shareware, 8
short int, 25
short-circuit evaluation, 117
signatures, 193
signed integers, 27
simple statements, 11
simulators, 237
single quotes, 69
size, variable types, 28
slash-star (/*) comment, 17
source code, defined, 8

space
   popped, 96
   pushed, 95
   reserving, 97
specialization, 249, 258
specifying classnames, 167
speed
   improving, using in-memory
      data structures, 268
   templates versus classes, 266
   timing code, 266
stack allocation, 96
stacks, 95
   versus heaps, 95-97
Standard C++, 7
Standard C++ class library, 179
standard output, 8
standards, naming, 171-172
state, 136
statements, 81
   catch, 42
   cerr, 39
   cin, 52
   compound, 11
   copy, 104
   cout, 15, 18, 22, 33
   debugging, 33
   if, 37, 81
      else, 41
      format, 38
   simple, 11
   switch, 81
   throw, 86
   try, 42
   using namespace, 16
static
   functions, 243
   initializers, 244
   local variables, 86, 90
   variable, 242
      in classes, 242
step (for loop), 91

stopping
   loops, 92
   programs, 71, 109
storage, 95, 97
   deallocated, 184
   storing named values, 270
streams
   closing, 137
   opening, 138
StreamTape() function, 138
stress tests, 225
string
   literals, 18
   terminator, 100
   variables, 28
strongly typed language, 6
struct declarations, 146
structure types, 126
   declaring, 126
structures
   creating, 127
   creating lists of, 128
   linking, 128
stubs, 237
subtracting operands, 109
superclass members, overriding, 211
superclasses, 206
   calling, 220
   testing using derived classes,
      226
switch statements, 81
   default case in, 82
symbols, validating, 200
syntax, enumerated types, 122

T

tape (calculator)
   reading from a file, 141-143
   recalling, 141
Tape() function, 99, 138

templates
    and speed, 266
    classes, implementation, 248
    code in header files, 249
    coding, 248
    declaring, 248
    definitions, 248
    header files, sample, 248
    inheritance, 261
    risks of, 262
    specialized, 249
    type parameters, 248, 261
    using, 248, 259
test harnesses, 223
    categories of, 223
    speed, 266
testing, 33, 111, 260, 273
    calculators, 109
    classes, 224
    for errors, 108
    for optimization, 263
    programs, 56
    regression, 32, 65
    for speed, 266
    superclasses, 226
TestOK function, 115
tests
    boundary value, 226
    capacity, 225
    categories of, 224
    empty, 224
    out-of-bounds, 33, 224
    performance, 225
    regression, running, 226
    running, 260
    stress, 225
    within-bounds, 33, 226
"the" (name prefix), 86
then keyword, 41
theThingWeAreDoing argument, 70
this keyword, 201
throw statement, 86

throwing exceptions, 44-45, 81, 86
time function, 266
timing
    code, 266
    determining needs for optimiza-
        tion, 267
true values, 38
truncation, 31
try statements, 42
try/catch, 70-71
type parameters, 248
    in templates, 261
typedef keyword, 132
types
    enumerated, 122
    structure, 126

U-V

UML (Unified Modeling Language),
    157
    attributes, 157
    class diagrams, 158
    classes, 159, 161
        anAccumulator, 160
        anExternalInterface, 160
        aRequest, 161
        aTape, 160
    datatypes, 158
undo, 270
unsigned integers, 27
user interfaces, 109
    anExternalInterface, 184
UserWantsToContinue functions, 69,
    73
using namespace statements, 16

validating
    functions, 116
    symbols, 200

values
  decreasing, 92
  false, 38
  increasing, 92
  returning, 18
  true, 38
variables, 23
  bool, 78
  bundling sets of, 126
  class-level, 243
  declaring, 27, 149
  defining, 24
  Dividend, 31, 51
  Divisor, 31
  global, 55-56
  increasing size of, 104
  int, 25
  integer, 27
  local, 56
  long int, 25
  names, keywords, 29
  ReturnCode, 39
  short int, 25
  static, 242
  static local, 86
  string, 28
  types, 24, 28
    in C++, 27
    size, 28
vector class, 180, 182
virtual
  destructors, 244
  functions, 235
    initializing, 230
virtual keyword, 154, 217
  destructors, 220
void, 51
  returning, 18

W-Z

walkthroughs, 116
weakly typed languages, 6
while keyword, 29
while loops, 69
  running, 72
  stopping programs, 71
whitespace, 17, 54
  braces, 17
within-bounds tests, 33, 226
wolf fencing, 225

zeroth character, 99
zeroth element, 99

Related Titles